Spelling Words and Sentences

for

Spelling by Sound and Structure

Rod and Staff Publishers, Inc.
P.O. Box 3, Hwy. 172
Crockett, KY 41413-0003
Telephone: (606) 522-4348

Printed in U.S.A.

ISBN 978-07399-0708-5

Catalog no. 160911

1   2   3   4   5   —   20   19   18   17   16   15   14   13   12   11

Spelling Tests

This booklet contains the words and sentences for the Spelling Tests in Rod and Staff's *Spelling by Sound and Structure* series for grades 2–8. The tests for all levels of each lesson are on a two-page spread so that the teacher can give the tests to various grades without needing to use several books. The review lessons require two spreads because of the greater number of spelling words.

Instructions and tips for administrating the Spelling Tests are given in the Teacher's Manual for each grade level. This information is not repeated in this booklet. You should familiarize yourself with the instructions before giving the tests.

Some spelling words, such as abbreviations, have special instructions in the Teacher's Manual. Because of the condensed nature of this booklet, such instructions could not be given here. These spelling words are identified with asterisks (*) with a note to see the Teacher's Manual for the special instructions. You should know what is expected in these cases before administering the test.

GRADE 2

1. *big*—We saw a *big* white cloud.
2. *fat*—Mother roasted the *fat* chicken.
3. *cake*—Pie and *cake* are desserts.
4. *rain*—God knows when to send *rain* to the earth.
5. *cap*—Hang the *cap* on the hook.
6. *days*—In six *days* God made the world.
7. *sick*—Some children are *sick* for many days.
8. *yes*—The opposite of *yes* is no.
9. *hat*—Who will bring Father's *hat* to him?
10. *word*—We will write one *word* at a time.
11. *ten*—The number *ten* is one more than nine.
12. *pig*—John feeds the *pig* corn and water.

GRADE 5

1. *probably*—The price will *probably* be the same.
2. *bananas*—Pineapples and *bananas* grow in South America.
3. *blooming*—The flowers are *blooming* nicely.
4. *command*—The farmer gave the *command* to halt.
5. *dismiss*—School will *dismiss* at three o'clock.
6. *knit*—Grandma wants to *knit* a sweater.
7. *false*—That was a *false* report we heard.
8. *nail*—Do you always hit the *nail* on the head?
9. *habit*—Start a good *habit* when you are young.
10. *apron*—Mother must mend her *apron* pocket.
11. *passed*—Everyone *passed* the test.
12. *breaking*—The sun is *breaking* through the clouds.
13. *treated*—Evil men *treated* Christ cruelly.
14. *sacred*—The Word of God is *sacred* to us.
15. *saint*—A true Christian is a *saint* on earth.
16. *entered*—The Israelites *entered* the Promised Land.
　　Five *animals* had come to the *stream*.
　　Carry the *basket* and pull the *hose*.

GRADE 6

1. *closet*—You should keep your *closet* neat.
2. *agent*—The real estate *agent* is here.
3. *insects*—Some *insects* are helpful to us.
4. *secret*—Many Christians must have *secret* meetings.
5. *blossoms*—The cherry *blossoms* are beautiful.
6. *couch*—You may sleep on the *couch* tonight.
7. *figures*—Be sure your *figures* are copied correctly.
8. *greetings*—Give my *greetings* to your parents.
9. *pennies*—Wasted *pennies* become wasted dollars.
10. *copies*—Please make two *copies* of this letter.
11. *plains*—The open *plains* were excellent pasture lands.
12. *degree*—The temperature was one *degree* above freezing.
13. *search*—The shepherd made a *search* for the sheep.
14. *taxes*—Our *taxes* are used to build roads.
15. *compass*—A good *compass* always points north.
16. *dash*—Put a *dash* of salt in the soup.
　　That *towel* has a pretty *pattern*.
　　Three *ladies* cut up *cabbage* for the soup.

GRADE 3

1. *ride*—Do you want to *ride* the horse?
2. *soap*—We wash with *soap* and water.
3. *finger*—Your index *finger* is next to your thumb.
4. *down*—The doctor walked *down* the hall.
5. *meat*—Please pass the *meat* and potatoes.
6. *pie*—Mother made cherry *pie* for dessert.
7. *fire*—A *fire* can't burn without air.
8. *neat*—Is your bedroom *neat* and tidy?
9. *lamp*—The woman lit a *lamp* and swept her house.
10. *town*—Jesus was born in the *town* of Bethlehem.
11. *button*—A *button* is missing on that coat.
12. *wide*—"Open your mouth *wide*," the dentist said.
13. *leg*—The chair *leg* is broken.
14. *key*—This little *key* opens the lock.
15. *mail*—Two letters came in the *mail* today.
16. *houses*—From an airplane the *houses* look tiny.

GRADE 4

1. *soup*—On a cold day, hot *soup* tastes good.
2. *grain*—Jesus' disciples picked *grain* to eat.
3. *west*—Grandfather lives a mile *west* of us.
4. *pump*—Do you have a *pump* on your farm?
5. *east*—The wise men saw a star in the *east*.
6. *study*—We should *study* to do our own business.
7. *hundred*—One *hundred* is less than one thousand.
8. *drum*—A large *drum* can be used to store feed.
9. *skin*—Did you ever *skin* a rabbit?
10. *windows*—We washed the *windows* on Saturday.
11. *until*—Everyone slept *until* morning.
12. *Bible*—The *Bible* is the Word of God.
13. *ready*—Ruth was *ready* to gather grain for Naomi.
14. *myself*—I can read the Bible *myself*.
15. *unless*—We shall go outside *unless* it rains.
16. *steam*—Water turns to *steam* when it boils.
    The *blind* girl did not see the *fence*.
    Copy the name on the *sack*.

GRADE 7

1. *brethren*—We need the advice of our *brethren*.
2. *enrolled*—Yesterday Kevin *enrolled* in our school.
3. *alley*—The narrow *alley* was littered with boxes.
4. *graduating*—Are you *graduating* from school soon?
5. *hungrier*—Soon James felt *hungrier* than ever.
6. *liveliest*—David's colt is the *liveliest* of all.
7. *listening*—Are you *listening* to this story?
8. *hoarse*—This morning I had a *hoarse* throat.
9. *briefest*—Tom's speech was the *briefest* of all.
10. *quizzes*—Brother Allen gave two *quizzes* this week.
11. *canceled*—We have *canceled* the meeting.
12. *engineering*—The bridge shows fine *engineering*.
13. *employees*—Only five *employees* worked Saturday.
14. *pulleys*—We lifted the heavy bricks with *pulleys*.
15. *straightened*—She *straightened* the tablecloth.
16. *shepherds*—Angels told the *shepherds* about Jesus.
17. *tariff*—The Dutch ship paid a heavy *tariff*.
18. *heretofore*—Everyone *heretofore* has had a cold.
19. *embargoes*—Nations often use *embargoes* in wartime.
20. *typewriter*—A noisy *typewriter* disturbs my nap.
21. *assure*—We *assure* you that we are honest.
22. *threaten*—Do not *threaten* to hurt your puppy.
23. *vice-president*—The *vice-president* spoke.
24. *vacancies*—The motel had only two *vacancies* left.
25. *children's*—Daisy was the *children's* pet goat.

GRADE 8

1. *inspiration*—Sunshine gives *inspiration* for a hike.
2. *exploring*—How about *exploring* some animal trails?
3. *initiation*—That was my *initiation* to wildlife study.
4. *justified*—At first Job *justified* himself.
5. *abhor*—Later he said, "I *abhor* myself and repent."
6. *contrition*—God honors such *contrition*.
7. *recovered*—Job *recovered* his former wealth and more.
8. *infallible*—God's judgments are *infallible*.
9. *reconcile*—Can you *reconcile* the conflicting reports?
10. *abnormal*—An *abnormal* rainfall ruined the asters.
11. *bumblebees*—Six *bumblebees* clustered on the insect trap.
12. *perished*—They *perished* in the fluid inside.
13. *materially*—The *materially* rich can be paupers in spirit.
14. *sincerely*—We should *sincerely* seek the kingdom of God.
15. *accordingly*—The rest of life will harmonize *accordingly*.
16. *unlikely*—It is an *unlikely* event that we will see a bear.
17. *alloys*—New *alloys* were used to build the barges.
18. *process*—The *process* is explained in this news report.
19. *overreactions*—*Overreactions* cause new problems.
20. *precaution*—A little *precaution* can save lives.
21. *secretary*—The school *secretary* filed the reports.
22. *engagement*—His new *engagement* was guiding tours.
23. *representatives*—Safety *representatives* visited the mine.
24. *fascinating*—I found a *fascinating* book in the attic.
25. *scheduled*—Sickness delayed the *scheduled* trip.

LESSON 2

GRADE 2

1. *can*—Lois thinks she *can* help us.
2. *tip*—We write with the *tip* of the pencil.
3. *man*—The name of the first *man* was Adam.
4. *bell*—Who heard the *bell* ring?
5. *yet*—Winter has not *yet* come.
6. *his*—The man waved *his* hand.
7. *bill*—Father paid the *bill* at the store.
8. *top*—Twelve is at the *top* of the clock.
9. *cat*—The mother *cat* washes her kittens.
10. *doll*—Let the girl hold your *doll* again.
11. *nut*—The squirrel has a *nut* between his paws.
12. *but*—We called, *but* they did not hear.

GRADE 5

1. *stepped*—The man *stepped* up to the door.
2. *manners*—Use good *manners* wherever you are.
3. *collecting*—His hobby is collecting stamps.
4. *fitted*—The puzzle piece *fitted* into place.
5. *common*—A cow is a *common* farm animal.
6. *topic*—Find a *topic* sentence in this paragraph.
7. *pity*—She took *pity* on the shivering dog.
8. *comfort*—Mothers can *comfort* crying children.
9. *comb*—Did you *comb* your hair this morning?
10. *barrel*—The big *barrel* has seed in it.
11. *carrot*—Bunny nibbled at the *carrot* I gave him.
12. *strain*—The extra *strain* on the rope broke it.
13. *clipping*—The barber was *clipping* hair all day.
14. *winning*—Who is *winning* the game?
15. *manna*—God provided *manna* for His people.
16. *trimmed*—The ten virgins *trimmed* their lamps.

    I had seen some *blood* on his *suit*.

    Set the *ladder* on this *heap* of dirt.

GRADE 6

1. *oyster*—Do you like *oyster* stew?
2. *wolves*—We saw five *wolves* in the zoo.
3. *beef*—That rancher raises *beef* cattle.
4. *factories*—Many *factories* make clothing.
5. *mercies*—The Lord's *mercies* are sure.
6. *vanity*—The Lord hates *vanity* and pride.
7. *poison*—Some books will *poison* our minds.
8. *invoice*—The package had an *invoice* inside.
9. *pavement*—The road past our house is *pavement*.
10. *native*—He was a *native* of Germany.
11. *prove*—Can you *prove* your answer?
12. *voyage*—Paul made a *voyage* to Rome.
13. *delay*—The snow will *delay* our trip.
14. *employ*—The company will *employ* more workers.
15. *battery*—There is a *battery* in the flashlight.
16. *choice*—Make a *choice* to do right.

    The man's *loyal* friend brought *groceries*.

    Will sharp *knives* help to *solve* the problem?

GRADE 3

1. goat—One *goat* had a bell on its neck.
2. trip—Our family took a *trip* last summer.
3. must—We *must* learn to follow directions.
4. rub—When you erase, *rub* carefully.
5. gold—Silver and *gold* are precious metals.
6. hit—I tried to *hit* the nail.
7. corn—Farmers plant *corn* in the spring.
8. Word—The Bible is the *Word* of God.
9. log—The old *log* was covered with moss.
10. hid—Mother Cat *hid* her kittens well.
11. tail—The horse switched his *tail* at the flies.
12. bag—Leave the *bag* closed for now.
13. roof—Rain pattered on the *roof* all day.
14. town—The stores in *town* close at five o'clock.
15. soap—Rinse the *soap* from your hands.
16. meat—What *meat* shall we eat for dinner?

GRADE 4

1. hammer—God's Word is like a *hammer*.
2. weeds—We pulled *weeds* in the garden.
3. kitty—Treat the *kitty* kindly.
4. beads—When the string tore, the *beads* scattered.
5. market—In Bible times, children played in the *market*.
6. bottom—The *bottom* of the bucket is rusty.
7. rod—Moses held his *rod* over the Red Sea.
8. heap—Mother gave me a *heap* of mashed potatoes.
9. papers—Keep these *papers* in your notebook.
10. rabbit—My pet *rabbit* eats lettuce.
11. arrow—Jonathan shot an *arrow* beyond the lad.
12. buggy—A horse and *buggy* passed our house.
13. roots—Tiny hairs on tree *roots* drink in water.
14. team—Grandfather plowed with a *team* of horses.
15. beans—Green *beans* give us many vitamins.
16. body—All parts of the *body* work together.

A *tiger* can *rub* his head.

My *puppy* sees a *penny*.

GRADE 7

1. decent—We expect *decent* manners at the table.
2. transfer—Ann will *transfer* her church membership.
3. passenger—The *passenger* train travels at night.
4. amateur—My father is an *amateur* artist.
5. employer—Ben's *employer* demands quality work.
6. infinite—Who can understand God's *infinite* love?
7. mediator—Jesus is the *mediator* between God and men.
8. authority—We accept the *authority* of the Bible.
9. treasurer—Uncle Henry is the *treasurer* of the board.
10. commence—The meeting will *commence* at 7:00 P.M.
11. synagogue—Jairus was a ruler of the *synagogue*.
12. superior—This story is *superior* to the first one.
13. circular—The planets travel in *circular* orbits.
14. cedar—Put the quilt into the *cedar* chest.
15. medieval—Castles remind us of *medieval* times.
16. director—Mr. Peters is *director* of the hospital.
17. particular—No *particular* person came to mind.
18. familiar—My horse knows the *familiar* road home.
19. initial—The *initial* cost was ten dollars.
20. medium—Is the coat a *medium* or large size?
21. aviator—The young *aviator* climbed into his plane.
22. initiative—A good leader has strong *initiative*.
23. finance—The *finance* charge was $450.
24. definite—Sarah could not give a *definite* answer.
25. business—Do not meddle into another's *business*.

GRADE 8

1. divinity—Miracles showed the *divinity* of Jesus.
2. exhausted—He became *exhausted* as any other human.
3. leisure—Jesus and the disciples had no *leisure* to eat.
4. suspicion—Walter Reed had a *suspicion* about mosquitoes.
5. swamps—He ordered the *swamps* to be drained.
6. ridiculous—Ignore his *ridiculous* comments.
7. theology—It takes more than *theology* to serve the Lord.
8. communion—*Communion* with God is important.
9. mutual—The *mutual* encouragement is vital.
10. abandon—Never *abandon* your commitment.
11. guarantee—God's faithfulness to you is a *guarantee*.
12. onion—Mother added *onion* flakes to the stew.
13. ruined—Susan thought it *ruined* the supper.
14. wretched—Perhaps she felt *wretched* from her cold.
15. necessity—Amos saw the *necessity* of organizing his closet.
16. bestow—He decided to *bestow* some things on his brothers.
17. underrate—Does he *underrate* the value of a keepsake?
18. temporal—Our *temporal* possessions will perish.
19. editorial—Printing goes faster than *editorial* preparation.
20. opinion—Every book reveals the *opinion* of the writer.
21. absolute—The frosty dawn broke with *absolute* stillness.
22. icicles—A fringe of *icicles* trimmed the balcony.
23. enthusiastic—My neighbor is an *enthusiastic* star gazer.
24. celestial—Orion strides along the *celestial* equator.
25. companion—Canis Major is his *companion*.

LESSON 3

GRADE 2

1. *map*—We keep a road *map* in the car.
2. *net*—Jesus told Peter to cast the *net* into the water.
3. *God*—The Bible says that *God* is love.
4. *love*—We *love* God.
5. *hill*—The truck drove up the *hill* slowly.
6. *jar*—The buttons in the *jar* are different colors.
7. *keep*—Where do you *keep* your boots?
8. *nap*—The baby took a long *nap* today.
9. *wet*—Everything is *wet* after a rain.
10. *seat*—His *seat* is near the window.
11. *mill*—The man at the feed *mill* works hard.
12. *met*—Father *met* the visitors at the door.

GRADE 5

1. *stiff*—Ruth has a sore throat and a *stiff* neck.
2. *bluff*—A *bluff* is a high, steep cliff.
3. *toss*—I will *toss* the ball to you.
4. *mass*—Along the fence grew a *mass* of tangled vines.
5. *sole*—There is a hole in the *sole* of the shoe.
6. *proof*—Do you have *proof* that you are right?
7. *tough*—The meat was too *tough* to chew.
8. *follows*—The earth *follows* its orbit.
9. *uses*—Mother *uses* milk to make pudding.
10. *cough*—When you *cough,* cover your mouth.
11. *scroll*—The man unrolled the *scroll* as he read.
12. *suits*—Yes, it *suits* them all to come.
13. *level*—The scales must be *level* to work right.
14. *press*—People *press* apples to make cider.
15. *soul*—Everyone has a *soul* that will never die.
16. *dwell*—Christians will *dwell* with God in heaven.
    The *total* number of *lily* plants is four.
    Bees *seal* the *cell* with wax.

GRADE 6

1. *bull*—There is a *bull* in that field.
2. *deal*—Laban made a *deal* with Jacob.
3. *moss*—The pioneers used *moss* for chinking.
4. *cliff*—The *cliff* overlooks the whole valley.
5. *grief*—Jacob suffered much *grief* over Joseph.
6. *drag*—Do not *drag* your feet.
7. *hem*—The woman touched the *hem* of Christ's garment.
8. *banking*—I do my *banking* in town.
9. *tongue*—The *tongue* cannot be tamed by man.
10. *hunger*—They had a *hunger* for the Word.
11. *lightning*—The *lightning* struck a tree.
12. *congress*—In the United States, *Congress* enacts laws.
13. *addressed*—This letter is *addressed* to you.
14. *credit*—Give a person *credit* for his effort.
15. *offer*—I made an *offer* to help her.
16. *labor*—It is hard *labor* to move rocks.
    Do not *linger* over your *duties.*
    The *final* cost was over a *million* dollars.

GRADE 3

1. *bit*—I accidentally *bit* my finger.
2. *dug*—Isaac's servants *dug* another well.
3. *fed*—Jesus *fed* five thousand people.
4. *rang*—The bell *rang* loudly.
5. *king*—Solomon was *king* after David.
6. *gum*—My upper *gum* feels sore.
7. *tag*—Is there a price *tag* on the coat?
8. *won*—Which team *won* the game?
9. *rest*—Mother wants to *rest* on the sofa.
10. *land*—On the prairie the *land* is flat.
11. *lot*—The parking *lot* is full of cars.
12. *bank*—Father cashed a check at the *bank* today.
13. *dust*—Sweep the floor and *dust* the furniture.
14. *must*—Someone *must* help him.
15. *lamp*—Light the *lamp* so that we can see better.
16. *trip*—Uncle Daniel's took a *trip* last summer.

GRADE 4

1. *smell*—Did you *smell* the smoke?
2. *sofa*—Father bought a *sofa* for our living room.
3. *pool*—The blind man washed in the *pool* of Siloam.
4. *ladder*—Jacob saw a *ladder* reaching to heaven.
5. *follow*—Christians *follow* Christ.
6. *suffer*—Jesus had to *suffer* much pain.
7. *seal*—We *seal* our letters before we mail them.
8. *field*—Ruth gleaned in a *field* of barley.
9. *stream*—A *stream* flows through our pasture.
10. *dollars*—Two *dollars* equal forty nickels.
11. *letters*—Write *letters* to your grandparents.
12. *loads*—Father *loads* the wagon with wood.
13. *wafers*—Mother gave us vanilla *wafers* for lunch.
14. *staff*—The shepherd carried a *staff* and a rod.
15. *tulip*—Jane picked a purple *tulip* in the garden.
16. *friend*—We love a *friend* in spite of his faults.
    She made her *pillow puff* up.
    This is too *dull* to cut a *loaf* of bread.

GRADE 7

1. *Calvary*—Jesus hung between two thieves at *Calvary*.
2. *fashionable*—Tea was served in a *fashionable* parlor.
3. *attack*—Our dog likes to *attack* woodchucks.
4. *sanctuary*—We entered the *sanctuary* reverently.
5. *condemnation*—Sin is under God's *condemnation*.
6. *freedom*—Anabaptists desired *freedom* of worship.
7. *Beatitudes*—Jesus gave the *Beatitudes* on a mountain.
8. *resurrection*—Jesus' *resurrection* gave hope.
9. *Gethsemane*—In *Gethsemane*, Jesus prayed alone.
10. *separation*—Hannah faced *separation* from Samuel.
11. *possession*—Never let a *possession* master you.
12. *machinery*—Heavy *machinery* rattled up the slope.
13. *discussion*—Class *discussion* was lively today.
14. *complexion*—Sue's dark *complexion* tans easily.
15. *worthy*—Only God is *worthy* of our highest love.
16. *suggestion*—Do you have a *suggestion* to offer?
17. *opinion*—In your *opinion*, which tractor is best?
18. *session*—The morning *session* seemed to drag by.
19. *indebtedness*—His *indebtedness* made him labor earnestly.
20. *Christendom*—Not all *Christendom* honors Christ.
21. *sanctification*—Jesus is our *sanctification*.
22. *confusion*—Dan's room was a *confusion* of clutter.
23. *sacrifice*—Job offered a *sacrifice* for his sons.
24. *worldliness*—Godliness and *worldliness* cannot mix.
25. *sacrilege*—Joking about holy things is *sacrilege*.

GRADE 8

1. *conjunction*—Use a *conjunction* in a compound sentence.
2. *omission*—The *omission* of one word caused confusion.
3. *precipitation*—A record amount of *precipitation* fell.
4. *accommodation*—The dam's *accommodation* is adequate.
5. *cancellation*—Icy roads led to *cancellation* of the meeting.
6. *caution*—Everyone warned us to drive with *caution*.
7. *elaborate*—Joseph gave Benjamin an *elaborate* meal.
8. *sympathy*—He masked his *sympathy* upon finding the cup.
9. *adoration*—Joseph really had *adoration* for his brother.
10. *petition*—Judah's *petition* freed Benjamin.
11. *biology*—We examined insects in *biology* class.
12. *classification*—Lewis knows detailed *classification* of bees.
13. *amphibian*—The salamander in an *amphibian*.
14. *graduation*—We saw the *graduation* from tadpole to frog.
15. *vital*—Exercise is *vital* to good health.
16. *vitamins*—The best *vitamins* are in fresh food.
17. *mortgage*—It does not pay to *mortgage* your health.
18. *application*—Do you have your job *application*?
19. *admission*—What is the *admission* fee per person?
20. *fission*—Nuclear *fission* is a result of nuclear reaction.
21. *biography*—The Bible is a *biography* of Jesus.
22. *immortal*—It is an *immortal* story.
23. *occasion*—The family sale was a special *occasion*.
24. *anticipation*—I could feel *anticipation* in the air.
25. *diary*—The dusty old notebook was Grandmother's *diary*.

LESSON 4

GRADE 2

1. *bus*—The driver of the *bus* is careful.
2. *cut*—Here is a scissors to *cut* the paper.
3. *did*—What *did* he say?
4. *feed*—We need more *feed* for the chickens.
5. *road*—Cars drive on the *road* every day.
6. *cup*—Please give me a *cup* of water.
7. *sat*—Mary *sat* and listened to Jesus.
8. *sad*—Mary and Martha were *sad* when Lazarus died.
9. *barn*—The cows go into the *barn* at night.
10. *feet*—Be careful, little *feet*, where you go.
11. *hook*—Hang your coat on the *hook*, please.
12. *dig*—The men will *dig* a deep ditch.

GRADE 5

1. *bishop*—Our *bishop* prays for us.
2. *scratch*—Do not *scratch* your chicken pox.
3. *machines*—A mechanic fixes *machines* all day.
4. *sandwich*—Did you eat my *sandwich* too?
5. *problems*—All *problems* have answers.
6. *motion*—Someone will *motion* for us to start.
7. *subject*—The storm was the *subject* of the discussion.
8. *mittens*—My *mittens* keep my hands warm.
9. *details*—He told us *details* of the happening.
10. *chicks*—Under a heat lamp the *chicks* are warm.
11. *sure*—Ivan was *sure* he knew his way home.
12. *ditches*—The *ditches* were full of water.
13. *shelter*—We ran for *shelter* when it rained.
14. *nature*—All *nature* shows that God is great.
15. *reports*—Book *reports* should be brief.
16. *tools*—Books are *tools* for learning.

Both *classes* used the *chalkboard*.
Many *churches* are across the *ocean*.

GRADE 6

1. *assist*—Will you please *assist* me?
2. *infant*—The *infant* lay in a manger.
3. *orchard*—Mr. White's *orchard* is for sale.
4. *leather*—The man wore a *leather* apron.
5. *length*—They walked the *length* of the street.
6. *method*—Which *method* is best for studying?
7. *beneath*—The shoes stood *beneath* the chair.
8. *priced*—The eggs were *priced* at eighty cents.
9. *increased*—Jesus *increased* in wisdom.
10. *required*—Mother *required* sugar for the cake.
11. *breathe*—Fish *breathe* through their gills.
12. *tithe*—Abram paid a *tithe* to Melchisedec.
13. *completing*—Are you *completing* your assignment?
14. *losing*—John is *losing* his grip on the heavy log.
15. *tickled*—The dust *tickled* his nose.
16. *securing*—The priests thought they were *securing* the tomb.

Therefore his desire could not be *satisfied*.
Mark looked *worried* as he was *studying*.

GRADE 3

1. *smile*—I like people to *smile* at me.
2. *slow*—We should be swift to hear and *slow* to speak.
3. *step*—The boy heard me *step* onto the porch.
4. *flat*—Lay the paper on a *flat* surface.
5. *pretty*—We saw a *pretty* sunset yesterday.
6. *frog*—Listen to the *frog* croaking.
7. *climb*—Be careful when you *climb* the ladder.
8. *spring*—Daffodils are *spring* flowers.
9. *grade*—You are in *grade* three.
10. *twins*—Some *twins* look very much alike.
11. *street*—The church is on the *street* next to ours.
12. *driver*—The *driver* in the other car waved to us.
13. *blue*—The boat sailed on the *blue* water.
14. *rest*—Jesus told the disciples to *rest* awhile.
15. *land*—Lot chose the best *land* for himself.
16. *dust*—The people washed the *dust* from their feet.

GRADE 4

1. *kitchen*—Our *kitchen* is a busy place.
2. *shells*—Jerry gathered *shells* of all sizes.
3. *flash*—What a big *flash* of lightning!
4. *classes*—We have two *classes* before recess.
5. *churches*—John Nolt preached at two *churches* on Sunday.
6. *match*—To light a *match,* use great care.
7. *peaches*—Ripe *peaches* contain vitamin C.
8. *pitch*—The ark was covered with *pitch,* or tar.
9. *cherry*—Mother made delicious *cherry* cobbler.
10. *branches*—Those *branches* are loaded with fruit.
11. *bench*—We sat on the third *bench* at the meeting.
12. *patch*—My coat has a *patch* on it.
13. *shape*—The cloud had the *shape* of a camel.
14. *cash*—Judas carried the disciples' *cash* in a bag.
15. *chop*—Our neighbors *chop* wood every Saturday.
16. *station*—We stopped at a gas *station* for gas.
Sweep the *ashes* off the *porch.*
A *beach* is a flat *shore.*

GRADE 7

1. *ignorance*—Through *ignorance* the damage was done.
2. *credential*—Education is a needful *credential* for a nurse.
3. *residence*—Do I call his *residence* or his office?
4. *nuisance*—Mosquitoes are a *nuisance* to us.
5. *admonition*—The minister's *admonition* is heeded.
6. *monitor*—Grandpa's heart *monitor* was stable.
7. *summon*—Please *summon* help right away.
8. *creed*—Can you explain your *creed* to an unbeliever?
9. *appearance*—We appreciate your neat *appearance.*
10. *cheerful*—Your *cheerful* smile brightened my day.
11. *monument*—A tall *monument* honors Washington.
12. *credible*—Can Matthew's strange story be *credible?*
13. *experience*—Job's *experience* of suffering purified him.
14. *attendance*—Was the church *attendance* large?
15. *ordinance*—Baptism is a God-given *ordinance.*
16. *emergency*—In an *emergency,* try to think calmly.
17. *independence*—America declared *independence* in 1776.
18. *conference*—I enjoyed the *conference* for poets.
19. *miracles*—Jesus did many *miracles* of healing.
20. *faithfully*—Jesus *faithfully* cares for us.
21. *who'd*—Linda was the one *who'd* been absent.
22. *confidence*—Gideon's *confidence* was in God.
23. *penitence*—Susan knelt in *penitence* and wept.
24. *fidelity*—Christians declare *fidelity* to Christ.
25. *credence*—Jesus' life gave *credence* to His words.

GRADE 8

1. *hangar*—A large jet rolled past the *hangar.*
2. *missionaries*—Ten *missionaries* boarded the plane.
3. *evangelist*—One of the men was an *evangelist.*
4. *pursue*—The Bible urges us to *pursue* holiness.
5. *desirable*—Meekness and humility are *desirable* traits.
6. *malice*—We must rid ourselves of *malice* and envy.
7. *counselor*—Jesus is a faithful *counselor* and guide.
8. *benediction*—The minister pronounced the *benediction.*
9. *auditor*—A new *auditor* checked the records.
10. *summary*—He gave a *summary* at the business meeting.
11. *beneficial*—The new tool proved to be *beneficial.*
12. *dictator*—The *dictator* grew more and more violent.
13. *advisory*—He needed a new *advisory* committee.
14. *malicious*—Three *malicious* men killed many villagers.
15. *mandatory*—It was *mandatory* to enlist in the army.
16. *auxiliary*—Fresh *auxiliary* troops were sent to the area.
17. *dormitory*—Monica lived in the *dormitory* three weeks.
18. *migratory*—Robins are *migratory* birds.
19. *customary*—It is *customary* for them to return every spring.
20. *commentator*—The *commentator* explained this verse.
21. *actor*—One little *actor* imitated the visitors.
22. *beggar*—He pretended that he was a *beggar.*
23. *laboratory*—We waited tensely for the *laboratory* report.
24. *benign*—The tumor was *benign.*
25. *malignant*—Mr. Smith had a *malignant* disease.

LESSON 5

1. *train*—What a long *train* that was!
2. *from*—We read *from* the Bible for devotions.
3. *sweet*—Bees make *sweet* honey.
4. *spot*—The dog has a black *spot* on his back.
5. *try*—Always *try* to do your best.
6. *stop*—Where should we *stop* to buy gas?
7. *black*—Coal is *black* and shiny.
8. *sleep*—Bears *sleep* during the winter.
9. *dry*—Use the towel to *dry* your hands.
10. *brown*—Most tree trunks are *brown*, aren't they?
11. *drop*—A *drop* of water fell onto my hand.
12. *green*—In the garden are *green* and yellow beans.

*See Teacher's Manual for special instructions.

GRADE 5

1. *library*—Isn't the book in the *library* now?
2. *honor*—God is worthy of all *honor* and praise.
3. *groceries*—Mother buys *groceries* at the store.
4. *supplies*—Cleaning *supplies* are in the closet.
5. *wrath*—"A soft answer turneth away *wrath*."
6. *bathe*—The boys will *bathe* their puppy.
7. *Sabbath*—Keep the *Sabbath* day holy.
8. *horses*—The galloping *horses* jumped the fence.
9. *honest*—Think on things that are *honest* and true.
10. *hours*—The clock strikes the *hours* all day.
11. *writing*—I am *writing* a letter.
12. *clothes*—Our *clothes* protect our bodies.
13. *thunder*—The sound of *thunder* scares our dog.
14. *dairy*—Conrad lives on a *dairy* farm.
15. *liberty*—You have the *liberty* to choose.
16. *valley*—A wide *valley* lay between the mountains.

A brown *turkey* scratched my *wrist*.
She is setting *another arithmetic* book on her desk.

GRADE 6

1. *chorus*—The class sang the *chorus* loudly.
2. *physical*—Jesus had a *physical* body like ours.
3. *paragraph*—Write a *paragraph* to explain your thought.
4. *telegraph*—The pony express was slower than the *telegraph*.
5. *nephew*—My *nephew* is five years old.
6. *typewriter*—Put this *typewriter* on the shelf.
7. *wrestle*—We do not *wrestle* against flesh and blood.
8. *introduced*—The teacher *introduced* the visitors.
9. *contrary*—Such an idea was *contrary* to the truth.
10. *represented*—Jesus *represented* the Father to us.
11. *approved*—"Study to shew thyself *approved* unto God."
12. *error*—A mistake is called an *error*.
13. *regarding*—Father was *regarding* the man seriously.
14. *replying*—I am *replying* to your letter.
15. *borrowed*—The widow *borrowed* jars from her neighbors.
16. *corrected*—Have you *corrected* your mistakes?

The *echo* seemed to *wrap* itself around me.
Mother *fitted* the *clipping* into her book.

GRADE 3

1. snake—We saw a large snake at the zoo.
2. size—What size shoe do you wear?
3. hope—I hope I do not get sick.
4. twice—Six is twice as many as three.
5. stove—In the winter the stove keeps us warm.
6. huge—Solomon built a huge temple.
7. wise—Solomon was a wise man.
8. bite—Take a small bite of food.
9. wave—A large wave splashed against the rock.
10. stone—Under the stone was a caterpillar.
11. stage—Have you seen the pupa stage of a butterfly?
12. rope—Children like to jump rope at recess.
13. zone—In the frigid zone the air is cold.
14. fire—Father started the fire with a match.
15. grade—In what grade are you?
16. smile—A smile looks better than a frown.

GRADE 4

1. stories—Jesus told many stories called parables.
2. another—God gave Jacob another name.
3. breath—We were glad for a breath of fresh air.
4. whose—A woman whose son had died came to Jesus.
5. chimney—The chimney is made of brick.
6. north—A dairy farm is north of our house.
7. together—Christians meet together for worship.
8. Bethlehem—To Bethlehem the shepherds hurried.
9. heathen—The heathen people do not know Jesus.
10. cities—Several large cities are in our state.
11. others—We try to treat others kindly.
12. whole—Mother canned whole tomatoes.
13. turkey—The wild turkey lives in the mountains.
14. families—People in families help each other.
15. thine—I am Thine for service, Lord.
16. berries—The berries will ripen in June.

Look south rather than west.

The soup may be thick or thin.

GRADE 7

1. desiring—At Pentecost, many were desiring baptism.
2. announcement—Your announcement surprised us.
3. pilgrimage—A Christian's pilgrimage ends in heaven.
4. development—A baby's development is exciting.
5. achievement—Reading is a big achievement.
6. solar—God created our immense solar system.
7. rural—They live in a quiet rural area.
8. adjournment—The adjournment is at a late hour.
9. consideration—Take facts into consideration.
10. diary—Never read a diary without permission.
11. calendar—Check your calendar for the date.
12. anniversary—My parents' anniversary is today.
13. perennial—Often, perennial flowers bloom first.
14. lunar—Have you ever seen a lunar eclipse?
15. annually—The trustees meet annually in April.
16. current—May I have your current price list?
17. management—Ben's choices show good management.
18. carriage—The polished carriage rolled along.
19. journey—Our journey to Alaska was interesting.
20. meridian—The prime meridian crosses Europe.
21. commitment—He made a firm commitment to Christ.
22. Colossians*—Paul wrote Colossians in prison.
23. Isaiah*—The prophet Isaiah foretold Jesus' death.
24. Jeremiah*—Some call Jeremiah the weeping prophet.
25. Thessalonians*—Paul exhorted the Thessalonians.

GRADE 8

1. countenance—Sara's countenance was all sunshine.
2. amusement—Her amusement tickled her brother.
3. livelier—Soon they had livelier antics.
4. vacuum—The noise of the vacuum cleaner ended the frolic.
5. acquaintance—It was special to renew the acquaintance.
6. extinct—We walked the rim of the extinct volcano.
7. chemical—A chemical explosion is dangerous.
8. biology—Planting seeds is a biology exercise.
9. geology—Many rock samples came to geology class.
10. bookkeeping—Who will fill the bookkeeping job?
11. preceding—Try to condense the preceding paragraph.
12. logical—Tell the events in logical order.
13. ample—We have ample time to rewrite the story.
14. exorbitant—Joel paid an exorbitant price for the cheese.
15. luncheon—They wanted it for the luncheon.
16. cease—Daniel did not cease to pray in captivity.
17. sacrilege—Did he see the sacrilege of the temple vessels?
18. Decalogue—Israelites held the Decalogue in high esteem.
19. theology—Their theology came directly from God.
20. apologize—It is honorable to apologize for your wrongs.
21. verbal—You need more than a verbal profession.
22. controlling—Who is controlling your thought life?
23. plenteous—There is plenteous grace for victory.
24. abstain—Let us abstain from appearance of evil.
25. compass—Warm fellowship will compass the faithful.

LESSON 6

*See Teacher's Manual for special instructions.

GRADE 2

1. *yes*—We answered *yes* or no.
2. *fat*—The farmer has *fat* pigs.
3. *big*—I like the *big* red ball.
4. *rain*—God sends *rain* to water the earth.
5. *sick*—Jesus made *sick* people well.
6. *bell*—The cow has a *bell* around her neck.
7. *doll*—Mother made my *doll* a new dress.
8. *cat*—Give the *cat* some milk.
9. *but*—The shirt was torn, *but* Mother mended it.
10. *his*—The carpenter did *his* work well.
11. *map*—This *map* shows the big rivers.
12. *jar*—Our honey *jar* is empty.
13. *hill*—The grass on the *hill* is green.
14. *seat*—Is anyone's *seat* empty?
15. *God*—In the beginning *God* created the world.
16. *cut*—Someone should *cut* the cake.
17. *road*—That *road* was full of ruts.
18. *sat*—The boys *sat* on the bench.
19. *barn*—Look for a red *barn* and a white house.
20. *hook*—Remember to *hook* the door to keep it shut.
21. *stop*—Cars *stop* at *stop* signs.
22. *dry*—We stayed *dry* under the big umbrella.
23. *green*—The rain made the *grass* green again.
24. *sleep*—Did you *sleep* well last night?
25. *spot*—The girls played in a grassy *spot*.

GRADE 5

1. *nail*—Find a *nail* to hang up this picture.
2. *hours*—There are twenty-four *hours* in a day.
3. *reports*—The class wrote *reports* about trees.
4. *press*—We could *press* the leaves in the catalog.
5. *writing*—Mother is *writing* a letter.
6. *sure*—The promises of God are *sure* and true.
7. *horses*—Six *horses* pulled the wagon.
8. *treated*—Abraham *treated* the strangers kindly.
9. *nature*—All *nature* displays God's handiwork.
10. *dairy*—We drove past a *dairy* farm.
11. *mass*—A cold air *mass* formed over Canada.
12. *level*—Hold the board *level* while you hammer.
13. *blooming*—Asters are *blooming* along the walk.
14. *proof*—This picture is *proof* that the earth is round.
15. *motion*—The officer will *motion* when we shall go.
16. *pity*—Jesus showed *pity* for the sick people.
17. *knit*—Some girls *knit* yarn into sweaters.
18. *common*—Washing dishes is a *common* task.
19. *tough*—The dog can chew this *tough* meat.
20. *sandwich*—Here is a *sandwich* for you.
21. *comfort*—The Bible gives *comfort* to us.
22. *Sabbath*—Paul preached on the *Sabbath* Day.
23. *bananas*—Buy some *bananas* for lunch.
24. *machines*—The *machines* made a loud noise.
25. *valley*—"We are going down the *valley*, one by one."

GRADE 6

1. *degree*—The *degree* of damage was not known.
2. *closet*—Paint the *closet* white.
3. *pennies*—Ten *pennies* equal one dime.
4. *agent*—An ambassador is an *agent* for his country.
5. *greetings*—Paul sent *greetings* to the churches.
6. *insects*—All *insects* have six legs.
7. *search*—Did you *search* for your book?
8. *couch*—We sat on a soft *couch*.
9. *compass*—Take a *compass* with you on your hike.
10. *taxes*—Publicans collected *taxes* for the Romans.
11. *beef*—That farmer raises *beef* cattle.
12. *voyage*—Paul's *voyage* to Rome was rough.
13. *wolves*—False prophets are *wolves* in sheep's clothing.
14. *vanity*—"All is *vanity*," said Solomon.
15. *native*—This is our *native* land.
16. *factories*—The *factories* are closed today.
17. *delay*—The driver could not *delay* any longer.
18. *poison*—Watch for *poison* ivy near that tree.
19. *pavement*—The *pavement* on this road is new.
20. *battery*—This *battery* is dead.
21. *cliff*—The sheep had fallen over a *cliff*.
22. *banking*—Father is *banking* the fire.
23. *bull*—The *bull* was behind a strong fence.
24. *tongue*—Guard your *tongue* carefully.
25. *grief*—The prodigal son brought *grief* to his father.

GRADE 3

1. lamp—The *lamp* will light the room.
2. town—This *town* has three grocery stores.
3. button—I lost a *button* on my coat.
4. pie—Cherry *pie* is my favorite.
5. wide—God made the great *wide* ocean.
6. rub—When we clean we *rub* and scrub.
7. Word—We love to read the *Word* of God.
8. roof—Does the house *roof* have a leak?
9. log—Please put another *log* on the fire.
10. goat—A *goat* can be a nice pet.
11. rang—We *rang* the bell at school.
12. fed—Have you *fed* the calves?
13. bit—Jerry *bit* into the apple.
14. lot—A *lot* of ducks are on the pond.
15. dust—Mary will *dust* the living room.
16. blue—The sky is very *blue* today.
17. driver—Who is the *driver* of that car?
18. grade—The fifth *grade* will write stories.
19. slow—Do not be a *slow* worker.
20. step—Do not *step* into the flower bed.
21. stage—A *stage* is a large carriage.
22. size—What *size* is your shoe?
23. stone—The great *stone* was rolled away.
24. huge—The *huge* elephant lifted a log.
25. zone—In the school *zone*, drive slowly.

GRADE 4

1. west—The sun sets in the *west* each evening.
2. body—An ocean is a large *body* of water.
3. north—Wind from the *north* is cold.
4. letters—Paul wrote *letters*, called epistles, to the churches.
5. skin—Gehazi saw that his *skin* was white.
6. another—The widow asked for *another* vessel.
7. pool—Jesus sent the blind man to a *pool* to wash.
8. pump—The plumber fixed the *pump* in the barn.
9. cash—She pays *cash* for groceries.
10. friend—"A *friend* loveth at all times."
11. papers —A pile of *papers* blew off the desk.
12. beans—We ate green *beans* and potatoes.
13. ladder—Jacob saw a *ladder* reaching to heaven.
14. grain—Father shoveled wheat into the *grain* bin.
15. classes—Spelling *classes* include taking tests.
16. kitty—Whose *kitty* is this?
17. bottom—Look in the *bottom* of your drawer.
18. cherry—Birds sit in our *cherry* tree.
19. arrow—On that map, an *arrow* points north.
20. stream—After the rain, the *stream* was high.
21. peaches—How beautiful the *peaches* look.
22. turkey—Mother roasted the *turkey* for dinner.
23. whose—A man *whose* name was Job lost all he had.
24. berries—"Can the fig tree . . . bear olive *berries*?"
25. buggy—Ann pushed her doll *buggy* on the porch.

GRADE 7

1. hungrier—What is *hungrier* than a bear?
2. graduating—Keith is *graduating* his papers.
3. vacancies—The sick pupils left four *vacancies*.
4. embargoes—Some *embargoes* do more harm than good.
5. brethren—Joseph was sold by his *brethren*.
6. pulleys—Levers and *pulleys* are simple machines.
7. briefest—My book review is the *briefest* of all.
8. quizzes—Beth liked to work *quizzes* and puzzles.
9. canceled—Linda *canceled* her dentist appointment.
10. tariff—Colonists disliked British *tariff* policies.
11. amateur—Albert was an *amateur* horseman.
12. mediator—Our *mediator* is Jesus.
13. employer—Glen's *employer* asked him to work late.
14. circular—Our weekly *circular* came from the store.
15. finance—The bank agreed to *finance* the purchase.
16. commence—The song service will *commence* at seven.
17. medieval—Many people were poor in *medieval* times.
18. initiative—Take the *initiative* in forgiving.
19. definite—Did they set a *definite* time for supper?
20. passenger—Wanda was a *passenger* on a jet plane.
21. sanctuary—A wildlife *sanctuary* protects animals.
22. worldliness—Selfishness reveals *worldliness*.
23. Beatitudes—Jesus spoke the *Beatitudes*.
24. separation—Milk *separation* was done by hand.
25. Christendom—*Christendom* is named after Christ.

GRADE 8

1. precaution—Take special *precaution* with poisons.
2. fascinating—Chording of music is a *fascinating* study.
3. abhor—Learn to *abhor* pride.
4. initiation—There was a short *initiation* assignment.
5. scheduled—The real work is *scheduled* to begin tomorrow.
6. reconcile—Can you *reconcile* the checkbook figures?
7. alloys—Many *alloys* are stronger than iron.
8. infallible—The conscience is not an *infallible* guide.
9. process—We will *process* your order immediately.
10. justified—Abraham was *justified* by faith.
11. bestow—What can you *bestow* on the orphan?
12. guarantee—Do you *guarantee* your products?
13. abandon—Cover the well if you *abandon* it.
14. underrate—People usually *underrate* the value of prayer.
15. leisure—All his *leisure* time is spent in gardening.
16. mutual—We bought the desk with *mutual* funds.
17. enthusiastic—Sandra is an *enthusiastic* baker.
18. ruined—Grasshoppers *ruined* the crop.
19. ridiculous—This is *ridiculous* weather for sledding.
20. divinity—Demons recognized the *divinity* of Jesus.
21. graduation—Regular *graduation* was seen in postage rates.
22. mortgage—His *mortgage* was almost paid.
23. amphibian—Put a little *amphibian* in your *terrarium*.
24. precipitation—Those clouds promise *precipitation*.
25. accommodation—Your *accommodation* was most helpful.

LESSON 6
CONTINUED

*See Teacher's Manual for special instructions.

GRADE 5

26. *clothes*—Hang the wet *clothes* on the line.
27. *dwell*—Some people *dwell* in tents.
28. *mittens*—Wool *mittens* keep my hands warm.
29. *winning*—Which team is *winning* the game?
30. *strain*—Did you *strain* your muscle?
31. *ditches*—Water from the road drains into the *ditches*.
32. *toss*—Did the boat *toss* among the waves?
33. *habit*—Saying thank you is a good *habit* to cultivate.
34. *passed*—Everyone *passed* the test.
35. *barrel*—The oil *barrel* is empty.
36. *topic*—Every paragraph should have a *topic* sentence.
37. *manners*—It is good *manners* to reply promptly.
38. *trimmed*—Last Saturday we *trimmed* the bushes.
39. *scratch*—Do not *scratch* the door frame.
40. *bishop*—Soon the *bishop* will preach a message.
41. *honor*—We are to *honor* our parents.
42. *library*—Where is the *library* book?
43. *comb*—Someone lost a *comb* on the driveway.
44. *honest*—Joseph was an *honest* boy.
45. *stepped*—Nora *stepped* onto the rug.
46. *collecting*—Philip is *collecting* stamps.
47. *sacred*—The Bible is the most *sacred* Book.
48. *probably*—We will *probably* clean the floor.
49. *groceries*—Mother buys *groceries* on Fridays.
50. *saint*—Every *saint* obeys the Bible.

GRADE 6

26. *drag*—Do not *drag* your chair.
27. *lightning*—Franklin invented the *lightning* rod.
28. *offer*—The men made no *offer* to help.
29. *addressed*—Moses *addressed* the congregation.
30. *credit*—Try to be a *credit* to your school.
31. *leather*—The lineman wore *leather* boots.
32. *priced*—This book is *priced* at five dollars.
33. *assist*—Allow me to *assist* you.
34. *breathe*—People with asthma cannot *breathe* well.
35. *length*—The whale grew to a *length* of eighty feet.
36. *required*—God *required* burnt offerings.
37. *orchard*—The apple *orchard* was white with blossoms.
38. *losing*—The clock seems to be *losing* time.
39. *tickled*—Mother seemed *tickled* with her gift.
40. *completing*—Jesus was *completing* God's will for Him.
41. *nephew*—Paul's *nephew* warned him of danger.
42. *chorus*—There was a sudden *chorus* of shouts.
43. *introduced*—Have you been *introduced* yet?
44. *contrary*—Jesus' life was *contrary* to the Pharisees'.
45. *physical*—Doctors give *physical* examinations.
46. *replying*—I am *replying* by telephone.
47. *telegraph*—Samuel Morse invented the *telegraph*.
48. *error*—There is an *error* in your spelling.
49. *typewriter*—Put the *typewriter* on the table.
50. *represented*—Candlesticks *represented* the seven churches.

GRADE 4

26. *roots*—"They saw the fig tree dried up from the *roots*."
27. *chop*—Mother wants us to *chop* the nuts finer.
28. *hundred*—A century is a *hundred* years.
29. *steam*—See the *steam* rising from the pond.
30. *weeds*—Jonah had *weeds* wrapped around his head.
31. *rabbit*—A *rabbit* was called a hare in Bible times.
32. *together*—Two men walked *together* to Emmaus.
33. *shape*—Aaron made an idol the *shape* of a calf.
34. *hammer*—No *hammer* was heard at the temple.
35. *unless*—We will come *unless* we call.
36. *soup*—Who wants tomato *soup* for supper?
37. *seal*—Do not forget to *seal* the envelope.
38. *breath*—God breathed into man the *breath* of life.
39. *branches*—All the *branches* are hanging low.
40. *stories*—Both *stories* were about blind people.
41. *match*—This sock does not *match* that one.
42. *patch*—Between the clouds is a *patch* of blue sky.
43. *staff*—A music *staff* has five lines.
44. *pitch*—Blow the *pitch* on the pitch pipe.
45. *station*—The train left the *station* on time.
46. *cities*—Those two *cities* are far apart.
47. *heathen*—Many *heathen* people have no Bibles.
48. *Bethlehem*—David lived in *Bethlehem* long ago.
49. *tulip*—Next spring the *tulip* bulbs will grow.
50. *Bible*—The *Bible* has sixty-six books.

GRADE 7

26. *discussion*—The *discussion* was on giving.
27. *sacrifice*—They sold their land at a *sacrifice*.
28. *confusion*—God brings order, not *confusion*.
29. *suggestion*—Glenn offered a good *suggestion*.
30. *possession*—Laban's *possession* was taken.
31. *nuisance*—Ants are a *nuisance* at a picnic.
32. *credence*—Paul gave no *credence* to wives' tales.
33. *admonition*—His *admonition* grieved the man.
34. *penitence*—With *penitence*, he confessed his sins.
35. *fidelity*—A good speaker system has high *fidelity*.
36. *summon*—Joe will *summon* me on time.
37. *appearance*—His *appearance* was neat.
38. *emergency*—Yield the telephone in an *emergency*.
39. *conference*—A *conference* is recorded in Acts.
40. *monitor*—I was *monitor* for the panel.
41. *carriage*—Grandpa had a tall, erect *carriage*.
42. *lunar*—Men visited the moon in a *lunar* module.
43. *achievement*—Man's *achievement* will vanish.
44. *diary*—Nathan kept a *diary* of his trip West.
45. *anniversary*—I sent them an *anniversary* card.
46. *solar*—Sunshine is the source of *solar* energy.
47. *consideration*—Joseph showed *consideration*.
48. *meridian*—The sun reaches its *meridian* at noon.
49. *Thess.**—Paul gives advice in *Thessalonians*.
50. *Isa.**—The prophet *Isaiah* foretold Christ's death.

GRADE 8

26. *immortal*—We follow an *immortal* guide.
27. *cancellation*—The lunch *cancellation* was expected.
28. *omission*—Do you mind the *omission* of a meal?
29. *petition*—An angry *petition* is not quickly granted.
30. *vital*—The victim's *vital* signs improved slightly.
31. *summary*—John prepared a *summary* of his sales.
32. *pursue*—It is vain to *pursue* happiness.
33. *desirable*—Contentment is a more *desirable* goal.
34. *evangelist*—The busy *evangelist* traveled widely.
35. *auditor*—An *auditor* needs complete records.
36. *malice*—"In *malice* be ye children" (1 Corinthians 14:20).
37. *counselor*—Choose a *counselor* who fears God.
38. *benign*—Our family cow is a *benign* creature.
39. *laboratory*—Please clean the *laboratory* equipment.
40. *migratory*—Can geese lose the *migratory* impulse?
41. *abstain*—You must *abstain* consistently.
42. *countenance*—Father's *countenance* told us his answer.
43. *apologize*—Be quick to *apologize* for an offense.
44. *logical*—The *logical* course is to repair the pump.
45. *luncheon*—We held the *luncheon* on the lawn.
46. *extinct*—Why is the passenger pigeon *extinct*?
47. *amusement*—A ripple of *amusement* passed over the class.
48. *acquaintance*—My *acquaintance* with him was brief.
49. *cease*—When did they *cease* minting one-dollar coins?
50. *vacuum*—Can sound travel through a *vacuum*?

LESSON 7

GRADE 2

1. *head*—The cat poked her *head* out the doorway.
2. *ever*—Has he *ever* been here?
3. *trap*—Mother set a *trap* to catch the mouse.
4. *dead*—She threw the *dead* mouse away.
5. *fast*—See how *fast* the dogs are running.
6. *left*—We *left* home at eight o'clock.
7. *egg*—Glenn ate an *egg* for breakfast.
8. *test*—We have a *test* every week.
9. *hang*—Please *hang* up your clothes.
10. *flag*—The red *flag* waved in the wind.
11. *glad*—The disciples were *glad* to see Jesus.
12. *said*—Jesus *said*, "I am the good shepherd."

*See Teacher's Manual for special instructions.

GRADE 5

1. *shepherd*—A good *shepherd* loves his sheep.
2. *wrap*—Mother will *wrap* the baby in a blanket.
3. *breast*—The chicken's *breast* is white meat.
4. *salad*—Carol made potato *salad* for supper.
5. *theft*—The *theft* was soon discovered.
6. *themselves*—The boys helped *themselves* to the cake.
7. *deaf*—Some *deaf* people talk with their fingers.
8. *laughter*—Hearty *laughter* is a good medicine.
9. *horseback*—John Wesley rode *horseback* to some meetings.
10. *twenty-five*—Uncle George milks *twenty-five* cows.
11. *forty-eight*—That city is *forty-eight* miles away.
12. *shadow*—When is your *shadow* longer than you?
13. *anywhere*—We can pray to God *anywhere* we are.
14. *wealth*—No one's *wealth* can buy salvation.
15. *cleanse*—The lepers wanted Jesus to *cleanse* them.
16. *eleven*—Joseph had *eleven* brothers.

Will you *address* this letter after *breakfast*?
Must I lay the pictures *against* the *background*?

GRADE 6

1. *defective*—The fire was caused by *defective* wiring.
2. *musical*—He seems to have *musical* talent.
3. *electrical*—There was an *electrical* fuse missing.
4. *electricity*—The discovery of *electricity* changed the world.
5. *domestic*—A cow is a *domestic* animal.
6. *correction*—Make a *correction* on your paper.
7. *publication*—This newspaper *publication* is free.
8. *construction*—The *construction* of a sentence is important.
9. *readily*—The children *readily* accepted the changes.
10. *stock*—We must *stock* up on food.
11. *attic*—Please shut the *attic* door.
12. *traffic*—The *traffic* was moving slowly.
13. *attack*—The Pharisees were ready to *attack* Jesus.
14. *automatic*—We have an *automatic* washer.
15. *public*—This was Jesus' last *public* discourse.
16. *successful*—We had a *successful* trip.

In one *stroke*, Saul lost the *kingdom*.
If you *knock* that down, you may *wreck* it.*

GRADE 3

1. *fence*—A wooden *fence* surrounds the pasture.
2. *stamp*—Place a *stamp* on the envelope.
3. *gift*—We will wrap the *gift* in pretty paper.
4. *handle*—The kettle is hot but the *handle* is not.
5. *hunt*—We must *hunt* for the missing shoe.
6. *copy*—Try to *copy* the words neatly.
7. *blocks*—Pick up the *blocks* from the floor.
8. *feathers*—Goose *feathers* make soft pillows.
9. *aunt*—Sandra's *aunt* is a schoolteacher.
10. *bread*—Mother bakes *bread* in the oven.
11. *bother*—Buzzing flies *bother* me.
12. *Son*—Jesus is the *Son* of God.
13. *build*—God told Noah to *build* an ark.
14. *hope*—We *hope* to see Jesus in heaven.
15. *wise*—A *wise* child obeys his parents.
16. *snake*—A black *snake* slithered through the garden.

GRADE 4

1. *heaven*—The stars are between *heaven* and earth.
2. *melted*—When the sun got hot, the manna *melted*.
3. *acted*—The opossum *acted* as though it were dead.
4. *dressed*—Abraham *dressed* a calf for his visitors.
5. *instead*—They use margarine *instead* of butter.
6. *death*—We need not face *death* fearfully.
7. *breakfast*—A good *breakfast* gives you energy.
8. *health*—Good *health* is a blessing.
9. *ordered*—Last week Father *ordered* a new suit.
10. *remember*—Jesus told us to *remember* Lot's wife.
11. *opened*—Samuel *opened* the doors of the temple.
12. *Ezra*—We read in *Ezra* of rebuilding the temple.
13. *Esther**—The Book of *Esther* precedes Job.
14. *Exodus**—In *Exodus* we read about Moses.
15. *Daniel**—The Book of *Daniel* follows Ezekiel.
16. *Genesis**—Read in *Genesis* about the Creation.
    Who *packed feathers* into this box?*
    Have you *planted* beans *again*?*

GRADE 7

1. *association*—An *association* bought our land.
2. *clamor*—Every morning the kittens *clamor* to be fed.
3. *professor*—A *professor* could answer the question.
4. *aboard*—Happily everyone climbed *aboard* the train.
5. *canceled*—School was *canceled* because of snow.
6. *assortment*—Grandma had an *assortment* of fruit.
7. *confession*—David's *confession* won our respect.
8. *admiration*—Job had a deep *admiration* for God.
9. *abroad*—Last year the Martins traveled *abroad*.
10. *earnest*—God answered Elijah's *earnest* prayer.
11. *accordingly*—It was rainy; *accordingly*, we played inside.
12. *hungrier*—The calves grew *hungrier* every minute.
13. *assumed*—Jerry *assumed* responsibility for the work.
14. *controlled*—We carefully *controlled* our experiment.
15. *appreciate*—All teachers *appreciate* smiles.
16. *accumulate*—Do not desire to *accumulate* riches.
17. *faint*—If you feel *faint*, lie down.
18. *attitude*—Your *attitude* speaks louder than words.
19. *administration*—The tyrant's *administration* was cruel.
20. *approximately*—We parked *approximately* in the center.
21. *parallel*—No *parallel* lines cross each other.
22. *arising*—Few were *arising* at six o'clock.
23. *proclaim*—Faithful ministers *proclaim* the Gospel.
24. *assignment*—Our first *assignment* was an essay.
25. *professional*—A health *professional* may help.

GRADE 8

1. *centipede*—A long *centipede* scurried into the crack.
2. *binoculars*—Morris followed the eagle with *binoculars*.
3. *procedure*—He dreamed of a *procedure* to capture the bird.
4. *obstacle*—An opportunity may look like an *obstacle*.
5. *carton*—Each *carton* holds twelve dozen pencils.
6. *abolish*—Abraham Lincoln meant to *abolish* slavery.
7. *instinct*—A robin's *instinct* tells it when to fly south.
8. *sketch*—This *sketch* shows the migratory pattern.
9. *peril*—Paul was in *peril* on the sea.
10. *abstinence*—After days of *abstinence*, God spoke to Paul.
11. *substantial*—There was *substantial* evidence of God's care.
12. *canvass*—Did they *canvass* the island for converts?
13. *cylinder*—A silo is a *cylinder*.
14. *biennial*—Nobody wanted to miss the *biennial* reunion.
15. *grippe*—Grandmother had the *grippe*.
16. *quartet*—A *quartet* of boys sang for her.
17. *devotional*—Father led a *devotional* from Psalm 23.
18. *desirous*—We are *desirous* to walk with the Shepherd.
19. *support*—Thank God for the *support* of friends.
20. *exhaust*—We shall never *exhaust* God's mercies.
21. *adolescence*—Skills learned in *adolescence* stick with you.
22. *deduct*—You may *deduct* ten dollars from the bill.
23. *unique*—This quilt has a *unique* design.
24. *octagon*—The darkest patches form an *octagon*.
25. *uniform*—All the curtains have a *uniform* pattern.

LESSON 8

GRADE 2

1. *show*—Will someone *show* me how to do it?
2. *then*—Wait until *then* to go.
3. *shall*—"Forgive, and ye *shall* be forgiven.
4. *three*—Daniel kneeled *three* times a day to pray.
5. *she*—Ruth said *she* would go with Naomi.
6. *cheek*—The nut made the squirrel's *cheek* puff out.
7. *this*—Is *this* your coat?
8. *thing*—The shiny *thing* was a needle.
9. *that*—You may open *that* box.
10. *chair*—Keep your *chair* legs on the floor.
11. *ship*—The people traveled by *ship* on the ocean.
12. *shed*—The door of the cattle *shed* was open.

GRADE 5

1. *image*—Adam was made in the *image* of God.
2. *penmanship*—We use good *penmanship* when we write.
3. *solve*—Can you *solve* the problem?
4. *solid*—The shovel hit *solid* rock.
5. *products*—They sell milk *products* in town.
6. *nobody*—The puppy had *nobody* to pet him.
7. *hospital*—The floors in the *hospital* sparkled.
8. *slippers*—Grandmother knits *slippers* for us.
9. *collar*—Mother sewed the *collar* to the shirt.
10. *message*—Brother Aaron preached a *message* on faith.
11. *cabbage*—The Millers plant *cabbage* to sell.
12. *post office*—I go to the *post office* for stamps.
13. *village*—On market day the *village* is busy.
14. *model*—The boy's *model* train broke.
15. *second**—One-sixtieth of a minute is a *second*.
16. *minute**—One-sixtieth of an hour is a *minute*.
   Would it be *all right* to use our gold *blanket*?
   Did that bird *swallow* the *grasshopper*?

GRADE 6

1. *industrial*—The United States is an *industrial* nation.
2. *misspell*—Do not *misspell* this word.
3. *embarrass*—The praise seemed to *embarrass* him.
4. *government*—The *government* needs our respect.
5. *syllable*—A *syllable* is a part of a word.
6. *synagogue*—Jesus went to the *synagogue* to teach.
7. *gossip*—Idle *gossip* does great harm.
8. *quality*—He has the *quality* of honesty.
9. *Gethsemane*—Jesus visited the Garden of *Gethsemane*.
10. *apostle*—Paul was an *apostle* called of God.
11. *inherit*—The meek will *inherit* the earth.
12. *customer*—Give the *customer* what he wants.
13. *chickenpox*—The baby has *chickenpox* too.
14. *everlasting*—The wicked shall go into *everlasting* fire.
15. *windmills*—Long ago, *windmills* were common in Holland.
16. *passover*—The *passover* lamb was killed and eaten.
   Roy found a *compass* at the *post office*.
   Will these *blossoms* make your *headache* worse?

GRADE 3

1. *tall*—Look at the *tall* grain elevators.
2. *supper*—After *supper* we always do the dishes.
3. *grass*—Cows eat *grass* in the pasture.
4. *dull*—Please sharpen this *dull* pencil.
5. *cotton*—A ball of *cotton* is very soft.
6. *dress*—In cold weather we *dress* warmly.
7. *puppy*—Whose *puppy* is barking?
8. *small*—A beetle is a *small* creature.
9. *penny*—The clerk gave me a *penny* in change.
10. *hell*—The ungodly rich man went to *hell* when he died.
11. *jelly*—I spread butter and *jelly* on my bread.
12. *cellar*—Water ran into the *cellar* when it rained.
13. *puff*—The steam engine gave a *puff* of smoke.
14. *pretty*—God gives flowers *pretty* colors.
15. *bread*—We need *bread* for sandwiches.
16. *aunt*—Are your uncle and *aunt* coming soon?

GRADE 4

1. *blanket*—A *blanket* of snow covered the ground.
2. *slipped*—The little boy *slipped* and fell.
3. *printed*—This book was *printed* in Kentucky.
4. *planned*—Mother had *planned* to bake today.
5. *dropped*—Sharon had *dropped* her scarf.
6. *minute*—Do you have a *minute* to spare?
7. *lock*—Please *lock* the door when you leave.
8. *visited*—Paul *visited* the churches he helped to establish.
9. *minister*—Listen when the *minister* is preaching.
10. *shipped*—The package was *shipped* to the school.
11. *finished*—Who *finished* doing the dishes?
12. *watched*—We have *watched* long enough.
13. *wanted*—Zacchaeus *wanted* to see Jesus.
14. *begged*—The lame man sat and *begged* for alms.
15. *doctor*—God gives the *doctor* wisdom.
16. *Dr.**—Do you know *Dr.* Nagle?
    Did *Miss* Esther bother *you*?*
    Will *Mr.* and *Mrs.* Daniel bring candy?*

GRADE 7

1. *liquid*—Any *liquid* can be poured.
2. *requirements*—Obey God's *requirements* gladly.
3. *observation*—Nature *observation* is rewarding.
4. *benediction*—A prayer of *benediction* was given.
5. *obedience*—True *obedience* comes from the heart.
6. *contradiction*—There is no *contradiction* in the Bible.
7. *inquiries*—Teachers answer many *inquiries* daily.
8. *oppose*—We must firmly *oppose* evil.
9. *controversy*—The *controversy* ended peacefully.
10. *procession*—The *procession* went to the cemetery.
11. *request*—King Solomon made a wise *request*.
12. *correspond*—Sarah and Judy *correspond* by mail.
13. *production*—Their milk *production* has increased.
14. *dessert*—Mother made a lemon *dessert* for supper.
15. *response*—The eager *response* cheered the teacher.
16. *devise*—Can you *devise* a better plan?
17. *pronunciation*—Proper *pronunciation* is good.
18. *requisition*—Queen Esther made *requisition* for the Jews.
19. *indicate*—Please *indicate* your choice of color.
20. *proposed*—Father *proposed* a plan to us.
21. *contrary*—Spot is our most *contrary* cow.
22. *indict*—False witnesses tried to *indict* Jesus.
23. *questionnaire*—Fill out this *questionnaire*.
24. *advertisement**—Leo saw an *advertisement* for a dog.
25. *examination**—Jerry's last *examination* seemed hard.

GRADE 8

1. *Pentateuch*—Moses wrote the *Pentateuch*.
2. *Decalogue*—The *Decalogue* is in the book of Exodus.
3. *elapsed*—Forty years *elapsed* in the wilderness.
4. *peculiar*—God formed a nation of *peculiar* people.
5. *breadth*—They filled the length and *breadth* of Canaan.
6. *compromise*—Joshua made a *compromise* with Gibeon.
7. *anticipating*—All the tribes were *anticipating* conquest.
8. *arguing*—God is not pleased when we are *arguing*.
9. *triplet*—This song has a *triplet* in the first score.
10. *mathematics*—The order in *mathematics* is very consistent.
11. *trivial*—A *trivial* mistake can be crucial.
12. *decimal*—Do you remember your *decimal* points?
13. *enormous*—One small error caused *enormous* loss.
14. *antiseptic*—Mother poured *antiseptic* on the wound.
15. *Antarctic*—Does the *Antarctic* Circle cross any land?
16. *glacier*—A *glacier* moves very slowly.
17. *protein*—That tan sponge is a skeleton of *protein*.
18. *kimono*—A flowing *kimono* dominated the Japanese exhibit.
19. *recognize*—God expects us to *recognize* truth and error.
20. *heresy*—We must be alert to avoid *heresy*.
21. *dual*—Emily travels freely with a *dual* citizenship.
22. *conveniently*—She can *conveniently* cross the border.
23. *aeronautics*—Each pilot took a course in *aeronautics*.
24. *duplex*—Our neighbors moved to a *duplex* in town.
25. *statistics*—Copy your *statistics* carefully.

LESSON 9

GRADE 2

1. *bunch*—We brought a *bunch* of radishes.
2. *both*—Roses and raspberries *both* have thorns.
3. *wish*—I *wish* I could see her more often.
4. *such*—Have you ever tasted *such* sweet berries?
5. *dish*—Grandmother gave a *dish* to each girl.
6. *bath*—A *bath* in warm water feels good.
7. *push*—Try to *push* the swing gently.
8. *brush*—Remember to *brush* your hair.
9. *with*—A cherry is round *with* a seed in the center.
10. *each*—God loves *each* of us.
11. *wash*—Naaman was to *wash* in the river.
12. *catch*—Peter tried all night to *catch* fish.

*See Teacher's Manual for special instructions.

GRADE 5

1. *thrust*—King Saul *thrust* a javelin at David.
2. *kingdom*—David ruled the *kingdom* after Saul.
3. *double*—You must *double* ten to get twenty.
4. *headache*—If you have a *headache*, drink more water.
5. *linger*—Do not *linger* at the door.
6. *anxious*—Fred was *anxious* to eat watermelon.
7. *stomach*—Does your *stomach* feel empty?
8. *couple*—We saw a *couple* of women there.
9. *utter*—She was too surprised to *utter* a word.
10. *junk*—They cleaned up the *junk* pile.
11. *rough*—The wagon bumped over the *rough* road.
12. *somewhat*—The air was *somewhat* chilly.
13. *shovel*—Thomas helped to *shovel* snow.
14. *understand*—Now I *understand* the problem.
15. *tablespoon**—Use a *tablespoon* of cocoa.
16. *teaspoon**—Put a *teaspoon* of salt on the corn.
    Should we give a *pint* jar or a *quart* jar?
    One more *ounce* will fill the *gallon*.

GRADE 6

1. *furious*—Jezebel was *furious* with Elijah.
2. *testament*—A will is a *testament*.
3. *generous*—Joseph was *generous* with his brothers.
4. *suggest*—Did you *suggest* that?
5. *chocolate*—We had *chocolate* ice cream.
6. *abundant*—God's love is *abundant* toward us.
7. *religious*—Jesus was crucified by *religious* leaders.
8. *Nazareth*—Joseph went from *Nazareth* to Bethlehem.
9. *according*—It came to pass *according* to the word of Elisha.
10. *territory*—This *territory* is unfamiliar to me.
11. *currant*—That is a *currant* bush.
12. *severe*—We had a *severe* thunderstorm.
13. *et cetera**—The words *et cetera* come from Latin.
14. *examination**—This *examination* is not hard.
15. *advertisement**—Put an *advertisement* in the paper.
16. *telephone**—The *telephone* is very useful.
    The first two months are *January* and *February*.
    He stayed with us from *September* to *December*.*

GRADE 3

1. *chicken*—See the little *chicken* on the roost.
2. *child*—Every *child* received a balloon.
3. *branch*—A swing hung from a *branch* in the tree.
4. *fresh*—We ate *fresh* peas for dinner.
5. *sheep*—One *sheep* strayed from the flock.
6. *showed*—Jesus *showed* Thomas His hands.
7. *rich*—Job was a *rich* man.
8. *beach*—All over the *beach* lay pretty shells.
9. *chill*—We *chill* our fruit in the refrigerator.
10. *wished*—Everyone *wished* that the dog would return.
11. *short*—Those questions needed only *short* answers.
12. *flesh*—Hawks eat the *flesh* of many animals.
13. *shoes*—Rubbers keep my *shoes* dry.
14. *supper*—What time is *supper* at your house?
15. *small*—This *small* notebook suits me fine.
16. *grass*—The dew on the *grass* was sparkling.

GRADE 4

1. *touch*—Feathers feel smooth when you *touch* them.
2. *blood*—Christ shed His *blood* on the cross.
3. *becomes*—A chrysalis *becomes* a butterfly.
4. *rushed*—The child was *rushed* to the hospital.
5. *trouble*—"God is . . . a very present help in *trouble*."
6. *covet*—We should not *covet* other people's things.
7. *punish*—Parents must *punish* disobedient children.
8. *country*—People move to this *country* every day.
9. *wondered*—Rhoda *wondered* who was knocking.
10. *says*—Jesus *says*, "Come unto me."
11. *Judges**—We read in *Judges* about Samson.
12. *Numbers**—Moses wrote the Book of *Numbers*.
13. *Proverbs**—The Book of *Proverbs* has wise counsel.
14. *Joshua**—Chapter 2 of *Joshua* tells about Rahab.
15. *2 Samuel**—We read in *2 Samuel* about David.
16. *1 Timothy**—Paul wrote *1 Timothy* to Timothy.
     Who *thinks* the *covers* are warm?*
     Mother *teaches* him to *button* his shirt.*

GRADE 7

1. *evidence*—His accusers found no *evidence* of evil.
2. *despise*—Jesus did not *despise* children.
3. *renown*—Moses was a leader of great *renown*.
4. *abnormal*—The spot was *abnormal* in color.
5. *dismissal*—After *dismissal*, Ruth walked home.
6. *visible*—Many stars become *visible* at night.
7. *abscess*—A painful wound may have an *abscess*.
8. *amateur*—Dale is an *amateur* wood carver.
9. *apparent*—It became *apparent* that we were lost.
10. *respectable*—Our homes should look *respectable*.
11. *spectator*—Lois was a *spectator* at the barn raising.
12. *absolute*—God's Word is *absolute* and unchanging.
13. *expectation*—We await Christ's return with *expectation*.
14. *appearance*—My *appearance* excited the birds.
15. *accomplish*—Linda could usually *accomplish* her goals.
16. *vision*—A blind man has no *vision*.
17. *principal*—The school *principal* is Brother Yoder.
18. *disappointment*—Samson was a *disappointment*.
19. *Beatitudes*—Jesus gave the *Beatitudes* on a mountain.
20. *discount*—Gary bought his shoes at a *discount*.
21. *visual*—A giraffe's *visual* ability is amazing.
22. *advise*—What would you *advise* me to do?
23. *inspect*—Mr. Smith will *inspect* our building.
24. *desperate*—He made a *desperate* attempt to escape.
25. *interview*—The board will *interview* the teachers.

GRADE 8

1. *synagogue*—Paul taught in the *synagogue*.
2. *magnify*—He sought to *magnify* Jesus as the Messiah.
3. *minister*—He could also *minister* to the sick.
4. *access*—Jesus is our *access* to God.
5. *security*—No insurance can grant *security* as Jesus does.
6. *atheist*—The *atheist* has a hopeless future.
7. *symptom*—Prolonged fever is a *symptom* of hepatitis.
8. *transferred*—A helicopter *transferred* the sick child.
9. *asphalt*—New *asphalt* was spread on the drive.
10. *disqualify*—Bits of chaff *disqualify* the flour.
11. *vaccine*—Is there a *vaccine* for malaria?
12. *quantity*—The temple contained a large *quantity* of gold.
13. *immense*—The pillars were *immense*.
14. *quality*—Everything showed good *quality* workmanship.
15. *magnificence*—The queen was awed by its *magnificence*.
16. *synthetic*—Do shoes made of *synthetic* material last as long?
17. *subtle*—Satan devises *subtle* temptations.
18. *microphone*—Is the *microphone* switched on?
19. *attorney*—Father asked an *attorney* about the deed.
20. *microfilm*—He located some *microfilm* documents.
21. *miniature*—We pored over the *miniature* pictures.
22. *maximum*—What is the *maximum* rainfall record for May?
23. *symbol*—Print the information beside the rainfall *symbol*.
24. *sympathetic*—Jesus is *sympathetic* to our human feelings.
25. *sympathy*—We should show the same *sympathy* to others.

LESSON 10

1. *shut*—God *shut* the door to the ark.
2. *sun*—God created the *sun* on the fourth day.
3. *little*—Zacchaeus was a *little* man.
4. *hot*—Corn grows in *hot* weather.
5. *bump*—The dogs often *bump* into each other.
6. *lift*—Can you *lift* the lid?
7. *son*—Noah was the *son* of Lamech.
8. *job*—Karen's *job* is to sweep the floor.
9. *milk*—Drink a glass of *milk* every day.
10. *pond*—Deer drink from the *pond* in the evening.
11. *hop*—The bunny went *hop, hop* down the path.
12. *front*—Someone knocked on the *front* door.

*See Teacher's Manual for special instructions.

GRADE 5

1. *priest*—Aaron was the first *priest* in Israel.
2. *thief*—One *thief* on the cross repented.
3. *receiving*—God is *receiving* praise every day.
4. *plain*—We ate *plain* cake without icing.
5. *paste*—You'll need *paste* for art class.
6. *handling*—He is *handling* the knife with care.
7. *explaining*—She was *explaining* the answer.
8. *weigh*—Who will *weigh* the bag of grain?
9. *straight*—Draw a *straight* line.
10. *speech*—He gave the short *speech* before we left.
11. *January**—New Year's Day is *January* 1.
12. *February**—Leap year gives *February* 29 days.
13. *March**—Each *March* brings us springtime.
14. *April**—Flowers grow in *April* showers.
15. *May*—Sunny *May* is cheery and warm.
16. *June*—The *June* sun helps to ripen strawberries.

Does he *preach* so that he *reaches* the heart?

I *believe* the name has *changed*.

GRADE 6

1. *pardon*—Please *pardon* my interruption.
2. *pigeon*—A *pigeon* is sometimes called a dove.
3. *fountain*—Jesus is the *fountain* of living water.
4. *principal*—The school *principal* took me home.
5. *principle*—The *principle* of honesty is important.
6. *rural*—Do you live in a *rural* area?
7. *articles*—These *articles* do not belong here.
8. *tabernacle*—The Israelites took the *tabernacle* with them.
9. *foreign*—Solomon had many *foreign* wives.
10. *Hosea*—The prophet *Hosea* lived in the time of Hezekiah.
11. *Nahum*—The Book of *Nahum* has three chapters.
12. *Psalms*—Much of *Psalms* was written by David.
13. *2 Corinthians**—Paul wrote *2 Corinthians* at Philippi.
14. *Philippians**—He wrote to the *Philippians* from prison.
15. *Philemon**—Paul's epistle to *Philemon* was a personal letter.
16. *Revelation**—The Book of *Revelation* tells of John's visions.

A *nickel* is made of *metal*.

Philip was a *deacon* who preached the *Gospel*.

GRADE 3

1. *pray*—We always *pray* before eating a meal.
2. *teaches*—The Bible *teaches* us how to please God.
3. *steal*—It is sin to *steal* time as well as money.
4. *grace*—May the *grace* of our Lord be with you.
5. *Satan*—God cast *Satan* out of heaven.
6. *obey*—"Children, *obey* your parents."
7. *deep*—How *deep* is the water in the pond?
8. *heavy*—The boy carried a *heavy* box.
9. *clay*—We like to play with *clay* on rainy days.
10. *shake*—Does the box rattle when you *shake* it?
11. *steel*—Mother uses stainless *steel* bowls.
12. *Easter*—The Sunday after Good Friday is *Easter* Sunday.
13. *piece*—You may have a *piece* of pie.
14. *sheep*—Hundreds of *sheep* graze on the hillside.
15. *tail*—The cow switched her *tail* at the fly.
16. *shoes*—Luke polished the *shoes* every week.

GRADE 4

1. *grapes*—Our purple *grapes* ripen in September.
2. *preach*—The ministers *preach* God's Word.
3. *reaches*—Our land *reaches* to that row of trees.
4. *raise*—Our cousins *raise* popcorn every year.
5. *shopping*—Mother went *shopping* on Saturday.
6. *cheese*—Eat *cheese* for a good source of protein.
7. *peace*—Great *peace* have they who love God's Law.
8. *painting*—Father is *painting* the barn.
9. *create*—On which day did God *create* the birds?
10. *Sunday**—A visitor preached *Sunday* evening.
11. *Monday**—Mother washes clothes on *Monday* morning.
12. *Tuesday**—Every *Tuesday* she does the ironing.
13. *Wednesday**—Last *Wednesday* we were at school.
14. *Thursday**—Thanksgiving is on *Thursday* each year.
15. *Friday**—Good *Friday* is before Easter.
16. *Saturday**—On *Saturday* we help to work at home.

Why did he *steal* the *clay* ball?*

She dropped the *heavy steel* pipe.*

GRADE 7

1. *moral*—Stealing is breaking a *moral* law.
2. *conscientious*—Joseph was very *conscientious*.
3. *prevail*—Goliath could not *prevail* over David.
4. *broadcast*—We must not *broadcast* a secret.
5. *kindergarten*—She taught *kindergarten* at home.
6. *document*—The *document* was signed by the mayor.
7. *prejudice*—Jesus had neither *prejudice* nor pride.
8. *acknowledge*—We *acknowledge* our weakness before God.
9. *northwestern*—Oregon is a *northwestern* state.
10. *high school*—Many students in *high school* study algebra.
11. *advantageous*—Typing is an *advantageous* skill.
12. *acquaint*—Did you *acquaint* yourselves with them?
13. *welfare*—The *welfare* of each other is our goal.
14. *antecedent*—Which is the *antecedent* of this pronoun?
15. *knowledge*—God's *knowledge* is past finding out.
16. *anteroom*—Susan left her coat in the *anteroom*.
17. *frequent*—Washing dishes is a *frequent* task.
18. *docile*—Old Bess is a very *docile* horse.
19. *separation*—We must practice *separation* from the world.
20. *conscience*—Our *conscience* pricks us at times.
21. *overlook*—We should *overlook* minor faults.
22. *doctrine*—All true *doctrine* agrees with the Word.
23. *conscious*—She was *conscious*, though badly hurt.
24. *farewell*—Simon bade his guests *farewell*.
25. *everlasting*—Jesus gives *everlasting* life.

GRADE 8

1. *chronicles*—Scribes recorded *chronicles* of the kingdom.
2. *curse*—Prophets declared God's *curse* on disobedience.
3. *apostasy*—His people had gone into *apostasy*.
4. *catalog*—I will share my *catalog* with you.
5. *manufacturers*—Both *manufacturers* offer similar products.
6. *circulation*—What is the *circulation* of the report?
7. *accommodate*—How many guests can you *accommodate*?
8. *category*—Divide each *category* into three types.
9. *apostrophe*—Use an *apostrophe* in a possessive noun.
10. *diameter*—Sam can accurately judge the *diameter* of a tree.
11. *employment*—He has *employment* at the sawmill.
12. *believable*—The beggar told a very *believable* story.
13. *bananas*—We found some cheap *bananas* at market.
14. *evident*—It is *evident* that they need to be used very soon.
15. *cataract*—My uncle had *cataract* surgery.
16. *significant*—Now he views *significant* stars clearly.
17. *apology*—We make no *apology* for living Biblically.
18. *modest*—A humble manner must go with *modest* apparel.
19. *moderate*—Keep the furnishings *moderate* and practical.
20. *ceremony*—The baptism *ceremony* drew extra visitors.
21. *speedometer*—The truck *speedometer* is no longer accurate.
22. *advisable*—It is *advisable* to get that fixed.
23. *candidate*—Each *candidate* will give a speech.
24. *address*—They usually *address* current issues.
25. *flammable*—We discarded the *flammable* drapes.

GRADE 2

1. *same*—Everyone had the *same* answer.
2. *nose*—Raindrops splashed on my *nose* and cheeks.
3. *slide*—You may *slide* on the sliding board.
4. *kite*—See the big *kite* up in the air.
5. *made*—God *made* the earth.
6. *date*—The *date* it happened was June 2, 1950.
7. *drive*—Father will *drive* the automobile.
8. *home*—We will be glad to go *home* again.
9. *dime*—A *dime* is worth ten cents.
10. *save*—Aunt Mary wants to *save* the stamp.
11. *bake*—We *bake* cakes in the oven.
12. *ate*—The birds *ate* all the corn.

GRADE 5

1. *cries*—God heard the *cries* of the Israelites.
2. *noticed*—God *noticed* Achan's sin.
3. *studying*—Were you *studying* for the test?
4. *throat*—Marlin's *throat* felt dry.
5. *aisle*—The center *aisle* is very wide.
6. *lining*—My coat *lining* is torn.
7. *dried*—Years ago Grandma *dried* apples to sell.
8. *height*—Whose *height* is four feet?
9. *lying*—The dog is *lying* beside the walk.
10. *satisfy*—He will *satisfy* his hunger with soup.
11. *July*—In *July* farmers bale hay.
12. *August**—The *August* days are often hot.
13. *September**—The month of *September* has thirty days.
14. *October**—Nights in *October* are cool.
15. *November**—The month of *November* has thirty days.
16. *December**—Last *December* was very cold.
    Find the *owner* of this blue *bicycle*.
    Who works with *poultry* the *whole* day?

GRADE 6

1. *museum*—A *museum* has many interesting things.
2. *design*—This is a good *design* for the house.
3. *dying*—The light was slowly *dying* out.
4. *groan*—The wounded man uttered a *groan* of pain.
5. *recipe*—Put the card in the *recipe* file.
6. *funeral*—We attended the *funeral* yesterday.
7. *bureau*—That *bureau* has many drawers.
8. *beautifully*—The book was *beautifully* illustrated.
9. *annual*—The board held its *annual* meeting.
10. *communicate*—Telephones make it easy to *communicate*.
11. *Jehovah*—The Lord *Jehovah* is our God.
12. *Messiah*—The Jews waited for the *Messiah* to come.
13. *supreme*—God is the *Supreme* Being.
14. *grateful*—I am *grateful* for your help.
15. *capable*—He is a very *capable* boy.
16. *loneliness*—The prisoner endured much *loneliness*.
    Has the number of *lightning* bugs *increased*?
    My *nephew* sends his *greetings*.

GRADE 3

1. *bright*—I shaded my eyes from the *bright* light.
2. *mice*—We heard *mice* running in the attic.
3. *blind*—Seeing-eye dogs help *blind* people.
4. *yellow*—Blue and *yellow* make green.
5. *grows*—Moss *grows* on the north side of trees.
6. *loaf*—Mother baked a *loaf* of bread.
7. *toe*—Did you stub your *toe* on the stone?
8. *pile*—On the table was a *pile* of clean clothes.
9. *bone*—Give the *bone* to the puppy.
10. *tonight*—Stars will shine *tonight* in the sky.
11. *might*—Yes, it *might* rain soon.
12. *woke*—A loud noise *woke* me.
13. *coast*—On the rocky *coast* stood a lighthouse.
14. *showed*—An angel *showed* John the New Jerusalem.
15. *Easter*—Jesus rose from the grave on *Easter* morning.
16. *piece*—Someone gave me a *piece* of paper.

GRADE 4

1. *invite*—Mother will *invite* guests for dinner.
2. *strike*—If someone harms you, do not *strike* him.
3. *shining*—The sun was *shining* brightly.
4. *float*—A light object will *float* on water.
5. *bowl*—We gave a *bowl* of fruit to Grandmother.
6. *oatmeal*—Did you eat *oatmeal* for breakfast?
7. *studied*—Martin diligently *studied* God's Word.
8. *tries*—Baby sister *tries* to walk.
9. *throwing*—The children were *throwing* the ball.
10. *sewing*—My sister is *sewing* a dress.
11. *closed*—Noah went in, and God *closed* the door.
12. *created*—God *created* man on the sixth day.
13. *changing*—Fall is *changing* to winter.
14. *tried*—Everyone *tried* to catch the rabbit.
15. *climbed*—Zacchaeus *climbed* a tree to see Jesus.
16. *hello*—We say *hello* to people we meet.

We *might coast* on the hill.*
Were *bright* letters put on the *pages*?*

GRADE 7

1. *dual*—Our tractor has *dual* wheels.
2. *admonition*—Ed's *admonition* humbled Sue.
3. *biennial*—Hollyhocks are *biennial* flowers.
4. *finance*—The company will *finance* cars for buyers.
5. *duplicate*—May I have a *duplicate* copy?
6. *proclaim*—We will *proclaim* a fast.
7. *biannual*—The *biannual* report was read.
8. *unique*—Penguins are *unique* birds.
9. *millipede*—How many legs does a *millipede* have?
10. *septet*—Seven people would make a *septet*.
11. *biscuit*—Would you like a *biscuit* with jam?
12. *triune*—God is a *triune* being.
13. *multiplicity*—She had a *multiplicity* of schemes.
14. *centipede*—Can a *centipede* crawl backward?
15. *sacrifice*—Abel offered a *sacrifice* to God.
16. *octave*—From low "do" to high "do" is one *octave*.
17. *century*—Nylon was unknown a *century* ago.
18. *vacancies*—Three *vacancies* remained in the motel.
19. *quartet*—The *quartet* of girls sang two songs.
20. *communion*—Our *Communion* is close.
21. *triplet*—Point to the *triplet* in this song.
22. *quintuple*—Please *quintuple* the recipe.
23. *decimal*—Move the *decimal* one place.
24. *semiconscious*—Mary was *semiconscious*.
25. *sextet*—A mixed *sextet* sang for Uncle Ben.

GRADE 8

1. *specific*—Father's *specific* directions helped us.
2. *cranberries*—Indians used *cranberries* for medicine.
3. *capacity*—The freezer is filled to *capacity*.
4. *formula*—What is the *formula* for mixing this spray?
5. *specifications*—Find the *specifications* on the can.
6. *specified*—Do we have the *specified* ingredients?
7. *detergent*—Use *detergent* when you wash up.
8. *typical*—Jason was not a *typical* guide.
9. *meteor*—His fame was like a *meteor*, bright and brief.
10. *arising*—Soon he saw complications *arising*.
11. *resign*—He chose to *resign* his position.
12. *eligible*—Is anyone *eligible* to take his place?
13. *specifically*—The manager *specifically* wants a young man.
14. *scheme*—Did your *scheme* work?
15. *deterrent*—Laziness is a *deterrent* to success.
16. *formal*—There will be a *formal* meeting.
17. *destructive*—Carelessness is *destructive* to friendships.
18. *deform*—Don't let it *deform* your life.
19. *structure*—Sentence *structure* affects the message.
20. *diagram*—Sometimes a *diagram* improves clarity.
21. *metaphor*—Find a *metaphor* in the first paragraph.
22. *target*—A writer's *target* is the reader's opinion.
23. *diameter*—A path runs through the *diameter* of the park.
24. *souvenir*—A small *souvenir* stand sits at the center.
25. *construction*—Road *construction* delayed our arrival.

LESSON 12

*See Teacher's Manual for special instructions.

GRADE 2

1. *fast*—How *fast* the train roared by!
2. *glad*—We are *glad* for sunshine.
3. *egg*—The hen laid her *egg* in the nest.
4. *head*—The cat rubbed her *head* against a post.
5. *said*—Someone *said* that it is raining.
6. *then*—Father went to the bank and *then* to the mill.
7. *chair*—Bring another *chair* to the table.
8. *ship*—The big *ship* sailed on the ocean.
9. *thing*—Where does this *thing* belong?
10. *cheek*—The teddy bear feels soft against my *cheek*.
11. *wash*—Remember to *wash* behind your ears.
12. *catch*—Try to *catch* the ball.
13. *bunch*—Mother bought a *bunch* of bananas.
14. *dish*—Grandmother gave a *dish* to each girl.
15. *both*—Bring *both* the bucket and the basket.
16. *little*—See the *little* red tomato.
17. *hot*—The soup was too *hot* to eat.
18. *sun*—The *sun* shone brightly all day.
19. *milk*—Here is a glass of *milk* for you.
20. *front*—Our visitors come in the *front* door.
21. *save*—You can *save* money by not spending it.
22. *drive*—We had a pleasant *drive* over the mountain.
23. *home*—How good it felt to be *home* again!
24. *made*—The widow *made* a cake for Elijah.
25. *kite*—A yellow *kite* was caught in the tree.

GRADE 5

1. *nobody*—I'm afraid *nobody* will come.
2. *anywhere*—Sheep follow *anywhere* the shepherd leads.
3. *somewhat*—The sky was *somewhat* cloudy.
4. *forty-eight*—After forty-seven comes *forty-eight*.
5. *junk*—Put this can into the *junk* barrel.
6. *plain*—The apron is *plain* green.
7. *teaspoon*—Put the *teaspoon* to the right of the plate.
8. *eleven*—Joseph had *eleven* brothers.
9. *kingdom*—The *kingdom* of heaven is for the poor in spirit.
10. *linger*—Do not *linger* when you have a job to do.
11. *shadow*—See the long *shadow* on the lawn.
12. *paste*—You may *paste* the pictures.
13. *August*—We have hot days when *August* comes.
14. *September*—In *September* autumn begins.
15. *February*—Whose birthday is in *February*?
16. *January*—The first month of the year is *January*.
17. *November*—There are thirty days in *November*.
18. *products*—Plastic and gasoline are two *products* from oil.
19. *solve*—Can you *solve* this riddle?
20. *solid*—Water changes to *solid* at 32 degrees.
21. *wrap*—We will *wrap* the meat well.
22. *straight*—Use a ruler to draw a *straight* line.
23. *priest*—Melchizedek was a *priest* of God.
24. *image*—The dog saw his *image* in the water.
25. *shovel*—Help me to *shovel* the snow.

GRADE 6

1. *attic*—The men were insulating the *attic*.
2. *stock*—You may put *stock* in her words.
3. *readily*—Jesus *readily* forgave the sinful woman.
4. *public*—Zacchaeus made a *public* confession.
5. *domestic*—The dog is a *domestic* animal.
6. *construction*—Steel *construction* is strong.
7. *defective*—Fred replaced a *defective* gear.
8. *successful*—Paul's preaching was *successful*.
9. *correction*—Make a *correction* in your books.
10. *electricity*—Hand tools save *electricity*.
11. *misspell*—Do you *misspell* many words?
12. *quality*—The *quality* of your work is important.
13. *industrial*—Ontario is an *industrial* province.
14. *synagogue*—Jesus taught in the *synagogue*.
15. *embarrass*—That did not *embarrass* her at all.
16. *apostle*—Paul was an *apostle* of Jesus Christ.
17. *chickenpox*—The baby has *chickenpox*.
18. *inherit*—The meek will *inherit* the earth.
19. *passover*—Christ is our *passover* today.
20. *customer*—The *customer* returned the goods.
21. *testament*—The lawyer wrote them a *testament*.
22. *suggest*—May I *suggest* a book for you?
23. *religious*—The Pharisees were a *religious* people.
24. *generous*—Boaz was a *generous* man.
25. *chocolate*—Do you have *chocolate* pie?

GRADE 3

1. *handle*—Can you *handle* the pony?
2. *fence*—A rooster sat on the *fence* and crowed.
3. *gift*—Your birthday *gift* was the pony.
4. *copy*—Can you *copy* this design?
5. *Son*—God sent His *Son* to die for all men.
6. *puff*—A *puff* of wind sent his hat sailing.
7. *cellar*—Our *cellar* is full of jars of fruit.
8. *dull*—Do not write with a *dull* pencil.
9. *penny*—"A *penny* saved is a penny earned."
10. *dress*—We *dress* neatly to go to school.
11. *cotton*—The *cotton* pickers worked hard.
12. *rich*—The *rich* man did not help Lazarus.
13. *beach*—At the *beach* people find shells.
14. *fresh*—The *fresh* air is good for you.
15. *wished*—Johnny *wished* he could go along.
16. *showed*—The teacher *showed* us a picture.
17. *clay*—The *clay* is brown and sticky.
18. *grace*—We ask God for *grace* to do right.
19. *obey*—Trust and *obey* God.
20. *teaches*—The Bible *teaches* us to be kind.
21. *deep*—God made the *deep* ocean.
22. *yellow*—Some flowers have *yellow* petals.
23. *blind*—Jesus healed a *blind* man.
24. *might*—It *might* snow today.
25. *loaf*—Buy a *loaf* of bread at the store.

GRADE 4

1. *becomes*—Taking tests *becomes* a weekly habit.
2. *wanted*—Zacchaeus *wanted* to see Jesus.
3. *closed*—God *closed* the door of the ark.
4. *blood*—Jesus shed His *blood* on the cross.
5. *hello*—She called a cheery *hello* as I passed.
6. *painting*—The men started *painting* the room.
7. *invite*—Open the door and *invite* the guests in.
8. *death*—Lazarus' *death* made Jesus sad.
9. *reaches*—One person's influence *reaches* far.
10. *grapes*—Grandma cooked *grapes* to make jelly.
11. *country*—Japanese live in the *country* of Japan.
12. *changing*—Jesus' first miracle was *changing* water to wine.
13. *created*—In six days God *created* everything.
14. *watched*—I *watched* for the mailman to come.
15. *cheese*—Slice some *cheese* for the sandwiches.
16. *tries*—Yes, the calf *tries* to walk but cannot.
17. *shopping*—Many customers were *shopping* early.
18. *begged*—A blind man sat and *begged*.
19. *punish*—God had to *punish* Achan for disobeying.
20. *minute*—"Just a *minute*," she said.
21. *ordered*—Mother *ordered* shoes from the catalog.
22. *shipped*—Grapefruits are *shipped* from Florida.
23. *climbed*—Green ivy *climbed* up the wall.
24. *float*—Did the axe head *float* or swim?
25. *sewing*—A man came to fix the *sewing* machine.

GRADE 7

1. *clamor*—Jesus hated the *clamor* in God's house.
2. *association*—We enjoy *association* with friends.
3. *parallel*—The boards in our fence are *parallel*.
4. *confession*—Achan's *confession* was forced.
5. *aboard*—Everyone *aboard* the bus seemed excited.
6. *proclaim*—He may *proclaim* it a disaster area.
7. *accordingly*—We saw bears; *accordingly,* we ran.
8. *controlled*—Ann *controlled* her impulse to laugh.
9. *professor*—Gamaliel was a Jewish law *professor*.
10. *approximately*—I need *approximately* ten.
11. *inquiries*—Jesus answered Nicodemus's *inquiries*.
12. *benediction*—After the *benediction*, we parted.
13. *proposed*—Three suggestions were *proposed*.
14. *liquid*—The volcano spewed out fiery *liquid* rock.
15. *controversy*—His miracles caused *controversy*.
16. *indicate*—Chills and fever *indicate* an illness.
17. *request*—Queen Esther's *request* was granted.
18. *correspond*—Lives must *correspond* with words.
19. *procession*—The animal *procession* entered
20. *response*—A plant moves in *response* to light.
21. *accomplish*—Did you *accomplish* much?
22. *disappointment*—A *disappointment* hurts.
23. *abnormal*—Albinos are *abnormal*.
24. *interview*—William's job *interview* took an hour.
25. *dismissal*—He got a *dismissal* for health reasons.

GRADE 8

1. *devotional*—The short *devotional* was very inspiring.
2. *obstacle*—The biggest *obstacle* is nothing to God.
3. *substantial*—A slate roof must have *substantial* rafters.
4. *abolish*—Can the law *abolish* crime?
5. *binoculars*—Focus your *binoculars* on the cliff.
6. *procedure*—Study the building *procedure* of the swallows.
7. *cylinder*—The *cylinder* is a common form in the kitchen.
8. *adolescence*—Important choices are made in *adolescence*.
9. *peril*—Beware the *peril* of wealth.
10. *exhaust*—We never *exhaust* Aunt Ida's stories.
11. *anticipating*—We are *anticipating* a long visit.
12. *elapsed*—Two years have *elapsed* since we were together.
13. *trivial*—Be alert to *trivial* signs of trouble.
14. *statistics*—Joan keeps careful *statistics* on her garden.
15. *peculiar*—Can you identify that *peculiar* odor?
16. *arguing*—Don't try *arguing* with the weather.
17. *breadth*—The *breadth* of God's love is unmeasurable.
18. *heresy*—A self-centered man is prone to *heresy*.
19. *protein*—Nuts and beans are *protein* foods.
20. *mathematics*—You must be awake for *mathematics* class.
21. *sympathetic*—Her *sympathetic* smile encouraged me.
22. *disqualify*—Dirty hands *disqualify* you for making bread.
23. *miniature*—The birdhouse is a *miniature* barn.
24. *access*—Faith gives us *access* to the grace of God.
25. *immense*—Solomon gathered *immense* stores of wealth.

LESSON 12
CONTINUED

*See Teacher's Manual for special instructions.

GRADE 5

26. *lining*—Mother put a blue *lining* in the jacket.
27. *lying*—A paper bag is *lying* on the grass.
28. *double*—Make the paper *double* before you cut it.
29. *rough*—The carpenter will plane the *rough* lumber.
30. *twenty-five*—A quarter is *twenty-five* cents.
31. *tablespoon*—We need a *tablespoon* in the fruit dish.
32. *studying*—We are *studying* our lessons.
33. *message*—Who preached the *message* at church?
34. *weigh*—These bananas *weigh* two pounds.
35. *collar*—The shirt *collar* rubs his neck.
36. *hospital*—The lady was in the *hospital* three days.
37. *thief*—Judas was a *thief* and loved money.
38. *receiving*—The man is *receiving* many cards.
39. *height*—It flew at a *height* of several miles.
40. *headache*—Has your *headache* gone away?
41. *stomach*—The esophagus leads to the *stomach*.
42. *anxious*—Father was *anxious* about the storm.
43. *satisfy*—Water will *satisfy* your thirst.
44. *aisle*—Do not block the *aisle* while you talk.
45. *understand*—I think I *understand* now.
46. *tbsp.* *—The recipe calls for a *tablespoon* of sugar.
47. *tsp.* *—Add one *teaspoon* of honey.
48. *Oct.* *—After September comes *October*.
49. *Apr.* *—One year we had a snowstorm in *April*.
50. *Dec.* *—*December* is usually cold.

GRADE 6

26. *abundant*—Christ offers us *abundant* life.
27. *territory*—That *territory* belongs to Canada.
28. *currant*—We had *currant* jelly in our sandwiches.
29. *principal*—The *principal* is not in school today.
30. *pardon*—The prisoner received a *pardon*.
31. *Psalms*—Asaph wrote *Psalms* 73 through 83.
32. *rural*—A city is not a *rural* area.
33. *fountain*—A *fountain* looks refreshing.
34. *tabernacle*—The ark was in the *tabernacle*.
35. *Nahum*—The Book of *Nahum* is very short.
36. *foreign*—Have you visited a *foreign* land?
37. *beautifully*—The birds sang *beautifully*!
38. *museum*—A *museum* is always interesting.
39. *groan*—There was a *groan* from the injured man.
40. *bureau*—I keep that in a *bureau* drawer.
41. *design*—Did you *design* this quilt?
42. *Jehovah*—The Lord *Jehovah* is our God.
43. *capable*—Mary is *capable* of helping you.
44. *dying*—We watched the *dying* sunset.
45. *supreme*—Jesus' sacrifice for sin was *supreme*.
46. *annual*—We had our *annual* school picnic.
47. *exam**—What day is our *examination*?
48. *2 Cor.* *—The minister read 2 *Corinthians* 5.
49. *phone* *—Our *telephone* is out of order.
50. *Rev.* *—The last chapter in the Bible is *Revelation* 22.

GRADE 4

26. *throwing*—Try *throwing* the ball straight.
27. *tried*—Satan *tried* to get Jesus to sin.
28. *peace*—"Live in *peace*," Paul wrote.
29. *breakfast*—Cereal is a good *breakfast* food.
30. *wondered*—The lady *wondered* where to buy milk.
31. *touch*—You will burn your hand if you *touch* it.
32. *raise*—Farmers *raise* crops in the fields.
33. *Friday*—Her appointment is *Friday* morning.
34. *Thursday*—They have a meeting *Thursday* evening.
35. *Tuesday*—Each *Tuesday* the baker delivers bread.
36. *Esther*—Chapter 1 of *Esther* is about Vashti.
37. *Judges*—Chapter 1 of *Judges* is about Israel in Canaan.
38. *Numbers*—*Numbers* 1 tells of numbering Israel.
39. *2 Samuel*—We read of David's kingly life in *2 Samuel*.
40. *Joshua*—Chapter 1 of *Joshua* is about Joshua.
41. *Genesis*—*Genesis* 1 is about the Creation.
42. *Dr.*—He went to see *Dr.* Snyder.
43. *Sat.*—The day after Friday is *Saturday*.
44. *Thurs.*—The day after Wednesday is *Thursday*.
45. *Tues.*—The third day of the week is *Tuesday*.
46. *Sun.*—The first day of the week is *Sunday*.
47. *Gen.*—The first book of the Bible is *Genesis*.
48. *2 Sam.*—After 1 Samuel comes *2 Samuel*.
49. *Prov.*—After Psalms comes *Proverbs*.
50. *Esth.*—After Nehemiah comes *Esther*.

GRADE 7

26. *advise*—Did you *advise* him to go or stay?
27. *apparent*—Rhoda's happiness was *apparent* to all.
28. *spectator*—Saul was a *spectator* at the stoning.
29. *expectation*—Planting brings an *expectation*.
30. *visible*—The accident caused no *visible* injuries.
31. *doctrine*—The Sadducees believed a false *doctrine*.
32. *acknowledge*—We *acknowledge* the truth.
33. *kindergarten*—Kevin is in *kindergarten*.
34. *advantageous*—Math proved *advantageous*.
35. *document*—A will is an important legal *document*.
36. *antecedent*—Greece was *antecedent* to Rome.
37. *prejudice*—Blind *prejudice* destroys friendships.
38. *conscientious*—He was a *conscientious* bishop.
39. *northwestern*—We took a *northwestern* route.
40. *conscious*—They were *conscious* of God.
41. *multiplicity*—God made a *multiplicity* of fish.
42. *biscuit*—A cracker is a *biscuit* in Great Britain.
43. *quartet*—Four people form a *quartet*.
44. *century*—Not many people live a whole *century*.
45. *quintuple*—If we *quintuple* two, we have ten.
46. *duplicate*—Pam had a *duplicate* key.
47. *septet*—A *septet* sang for Lois.
48. *millipede*—The *millipede* scared her.
49. *unique*—The rock was *unique*.
50. *triune*—We worship a *triune* God.

GRADE 8

26. *symptom*—Failing vision is a *symptom* of old age.
27. *asphalt*—Utah has natural *asphalt* deposits.
28. *maximum*—What is the *maximum* yield per acre of corn?
29. *security*—There is no *security* in money.
30. *subtle*—Praise of men is a *subtle* snare.
31. *category*—This poem fits in the narrative *category*.
32. *employment*—Many lost *employment* in the Depression.
33. *accommodate*—Would that hole *accommodate* a fox?
34. *apostrophe*—Place your *apostrophe* high enough to be clear.
35. *manufacturers*—Why do *manufacturers* advertise?
36. *modest*—One good advertisement is *modest* pricing.
37. *apology*—Accept my *apology* for the mistake.
38. *advisable*—When is it *advisable* to prune the trees?
39. *catalog*—A card *catalog* lists each book three ways.
40. *significant*—Each way has a *significant* purpose.
41. *capacity*—Sorrow increases your *capacity* for joy.
42. *detergent*—This *detergent* gives me a rash.
43. *formula*—What is your *formula* for friendship?
44. *resign*—A true friend will *resign* some preferences.
45. *specifically*—David *specifically* requested direction.
46. *meteor*—We enjoyed the *meteor* shower in August.
47. *target*—The Christian is a *target* for ridicule.
48. *destructive*—Worry is as *destructive* as cancer.
49. *souvenir*—Leon's scar is a *souvenir* of his camel ride.
50. *eligible*—No one was *eligible* for typing class.

LESSON 13

1. *heads*—Only their *heads* showed above the tall grass.
2. *beds*—Two *beds* are in the bedroom.
3. *girls*—Many *girls* like to sew.
4. *birds*—Listen to the *birds* sing.
5. *arms*—His *arms* were tired from working.
6. *seats*—All the *seats* were full.
7. *roads*—The map shows which *roads* to drive.
8. *trains*—Two *trains* stopped at the station.
9. *trees*—Pine *trees* have narrow needles.
10. *boys*—Some of the *boys* played tag.
11. *bees*—The *bees* make honey for us.
12. *rooms*—How many *rooms* are in your house?

*See Teacher's Manual for special instructions.

GRADE 5

1. *group*—A *group* of people sang for the sick man.
2. *avenue*—Follow this *avenue* to the park.
3. *strongest*—Which table has the *strongest* legs?
4. *rude*—Never be *rude* to anyone.
5. *view*—We had a lovely *view* from the hilltop.
6. *fuel*—Automobiles need *fuel* to run.
7. *tight*—The child held *tight* to his mother.
8. *unit*—We took the *unit* test last week.
9. *refused*—The man *refused* to take the tract.
10. *beauty*—Let the *beauty* of Jesus be seen in you.
11. *whom*—To *whom* do you go when you are in trouble?
12. *loose*—Do you let your dog run *loose* at home?
13. *Hebrews**—The Book of *Hebrews* has thirteen chapters.
14. *Romans**—The Book of *Romans* was written by Paul.
15. *Titus**—Paul wrote to *Titus,* his fellow laborer.
16. *Matthew**—*Matthew* is the first Gospel.
    Mother was lying in bed all of *Sunday* and *Monday.*
    She could sit up again on *Tuesday* and *Wednesday.*

GRADE 6

1. *league*—Joshua made a *league* with the Gibeonites.
2. *deceive*—We must not *deceive* others.
3. *grieve*—Do not *grieve* your parents.
4. *weight*—The *weight* of the truck was ten tons.
5. *depot*—We stopped at the bus *depot* in town.
6. *ceiling*—Can you reach the *ceiling?*
7. *relief*—It was a *relief* to hear your voice.
8. *apiece*—The books cost one dollar *apiece.*
9. *shield*—The Lord is my *shield* and buckler.
10. *veil*—Moses put a *veil* over his face.
11. *cedar*—The *cedar* tree is an evergreen.
12. *believed*—They *believed* and were baptized.
13. *unbeliever*—An *unbeliever* will not enter heaven.
14. *medium*—Set it on *medium* heat.
15. *reindeer*—There are *reindeer* in Norway.
16. *children's*—The *children's* books are over here.
    It is hard to *breathe* at this *height.*
    Neither of these facts is a *secret.*

GRADE 3

1. *things*—Twelve *things* make a dozen.
2. *thick*—The butcher cut a *thick* slice of ham.
3. *rather*—The air was *rather* cool.
4. *these*—Someone may eat *these* apples.
5. *thine*—We pray, "For *thine* is the kingdom."
6. *thankful*—Let us be *thankful* for our blessings.
7. *path*—A narrow *path* led to the door.
8. *thinks*—No one *thinks* he lost that button.
9. *girl's*—I forgot the *girl's* name.
10. *father's*—Your *father's* work is interesting.
11. *mother's*—You can be your *mother's* helper.
12. *man's*—Hand the *man's* hat to him.
13. *teacher's*—The *teacher's* lunch box was green.
14. *frog*—Did you hear the *frog* croaking?
15. *chicken*—The smallest *chicken* ate most of the grain.
16. *tonight*—Is *tonight* the night for the song service?

GRADE 4

1. *few*—Jesus fed the people with only a *few* loaves.
2. *lowest*—The *lowest* line on the music staff is E.
3. *finest*—I used the pen with the *finest* point.
4. *highway*—A *highway* is named for Queen Elizabeth.
5. *largest*—The Pacific is the *largest* ocean.
6. *moonlight*—Leon ran by *moonlight* to the barn.
7. *schoolhouse*—He fixed the *schoolhouse* door.
8. *greatest*—"He that is *greatest* . . . shall be your servant."
9. *mule*—Listen to the *mule* braying.
10. *smooth*—Babine Lake is *smooth* in the morning.
11. *through*—In heaven, thieves do not break *through*.
12. *threw*—Kenneth *threw* away the wrapper.
13. *later*—It may be *later* than you think.
14. *tune*—We sang the same *tune* for both songs.
15. *sooner*—Kathy finished *sooner* than I did.
16. *goose*—The roast *goose* smells delicious.

A *tooth* of the saw *flew* across the room.*
The *truth* is that Jesus left the *tomb*.*

GRADE 7

1. *marvelous*—What a *marvelous* God we serve!
2. *promotion*—David accepted his *promotion* to be king.
3. *religious*—Saul was very *religious* before his conversion.
4. *activity*—The kitchen was a beehive of *activity*.
5. *mischievous*—Mark flashed a *mischievous* grin.
6. *thorough*—Thomas did a *thorough* job of weeding.
7. *actor*—An *actor* works on a stage.
8. *mobile*—A trailer is called a *mobile* home.
9. *verbose*—Some writing is *verbose* and meaningless.
10. *agency*—The travel *agency* sent a letter today.
11. *motivate*—Your enthusiasm can *motivate* others.
12. *virtuous*—Solomon described a *virtuous* woman.
13. *agenda*—What is on your *agenda* for today?
14. *movement*—Allen saw a *movement* in the bushes.
15. *confidence*—Jonathan had *confidence* in David.
16. *agitate*—Do not *agitate* the dog unnecessarily.
17. *mysterious*—What made that *mysterious* footprint?
18. *grease*—The bacon *grease* sputtered in the pan.
19. *defense*—Paul made his *defense* to King Agrippa.
20. *poisonous*—Turpentine is *poisonous* if swallowed.
21. *initial*—Write only your first *initial* here.
22. *gracious*—Aunt Jane is a very *gracious* hostess.
23. *prairie*—The rolling *prairie* has few trees.
24. *mediator*—Two estranged friends needed a *mediator*.
25. *license*—The bakery's *license* must be renewed.

GRADE 8

1. *apostolic*—Peter was one of the *apostolic* leaders.
2. *characteristic*—His impulsive *characteristic* led to grief.
3. *acknowledgment*—His *acknowledgment* of error was clear.
4. *jealous*—God is *jealous* over us.
5. *assurance*—We have *assurance* of His protection.
6. *heroic*—Joseph is a *heroic* example of faithfulness.
7. *certify*—You must *certify* ownership to cross the border.
8. *consultation*—An officer held a *consultation* with the men.
9. *financial*—Some *financial* needs were evident.
10. *approximately*—They paid *approximately* twenty dollars.
11. *ascertain*—Can you *ascertain* the flavor in this cookie?
12. *dramatic*—There was *dramatic* improvement overnight.
13. *athletic*—Studies come ahead of *athletic* events.
14. *artistic*—Practice develops *artistic* skill.
15. *element*—C is the symbol for the *element* carbon.
16. *cosmic*—Scientists measured *cosmic* rays.
17. *certificate*—Gayle's *certificate* rewards perfect attendance.
18. *musical*—Howard talks in *musical* tones.
19. *noticeable*—A *noticeable* tiredness came over him.
20. *crisis*—A health *crisis* was evident.
21. *intestine*—Blockage of the *intestine* could be fatal.
22. *cardiac*—The *cardiac* muscle pumps a gallon a minute.
23. *discord*—Do not sow *discord* among brethren.
24. *potatoes*—Dwayne likes *potatoes* with gravy.
25. *colonel*—A young *colonel* examined the draftees.

LESSON 14

GRADE 2

1. *baby*—Moses' mother put her *baby* into a basket.
2. *names*—The Bible gives many *names* for Jesus.
3. *times*—Peter denied Jesus three *times*.
4. *babies*—Both *babies* are sleeping.
5. *cows*—In the barn are *cows* and chickens.
6. *lines*—Are the *lines* straight or crooked?
7. *party*—At our *party* we had milk and crackers.
8. *bushes*—A row of *bushes* is beside the house.
9. *parties*—The girls have *parties* with their dolls.
10. *houses*—Some *houses* are made of brick.
11. *nights*—For two *nights* they slept away from home.
12. *kisses*—When the baby cries, the mother *kisses* him.

GRADE 5

1. *sermon*—What was the *sermon* about?
2. *firm*—A house needs a *firm* foundation.
3. *earliest*—The *earliest* bird gets the worm.
4. *easier*—Some words are *easier* to spell than others.
5. *worried*—She was *worried* that she would get sick.
6. *purse*—A *purse* is for carrying money.
7. *curtain*—Mother hung a *curtain* at the window.
8. *circle*—The airplane made a *circle* before it landed.
9. *purple*—The king wore a *purple* robe.
10. *worship*—We can *worship* God here at school.
11. *windy*—Was it *windy* last evening?
12. *stern*—The judge had a *stern* look.
13. *worse*—His cold is *worse* today.
14. *worst*—That was the *worst* storm we ever had.
15. *perfect*—Jesus is our *perfect* example.
16. *serve*—Daniel was not afraid to *serve* God.
    Had they gone *earlier* than *Friday*?
    No girls helped from *Thursday* to *Saturday*.

GRADE 6

1. *surface*—A whale must *surface* for air.
2. *burden*—Jesus is our *burden* bearer.
3. *courtesy*—Please show *courtesy* to your guests.
4. *earnest*—He is an *earnest* young man.
5. *circulation*—Grandmother's *circulation* is poor.
6. *eternal*—We have God's *eternal* Word.
7. *firmament*—The *firmament* was made on the second day.
8. *personality*—Her *personality* seems very pleasant.
9. *research*—Have you done your *research* properly?
10. *current*—The *current* is strong close to the shore.
11. *reverse*—You must *reverse* your thinking.
12. *reserve*—Please *reserve* this seat.
13. *furnace*—The *furnace* is hot.
14. *missionary*—I like to read *missionary* stories.
15. *merchant*—That is a *merchant* ship.
16. *servant*—The minister is a *servant* of God.
    Is man the *worst* enemy of *alligators*?
    My *sister's* class will *worship* here.

GRADE 3

1. *covers*—A cloud often *covers* the mountaintop.
2. *sisters*—How many *sisters* do you have?
3. *bones*—You have three *bones* in each finger.
4. *ashes*—A pile of *ashes* remained from the fire.
5. *pages*—The girl read four *pages* of the book.
6. *legs*—Those stockings should keep your *legs* warm.
7. *gifts*—All the *gifts* are for the sick child.
8. *face*—Be sure your *face* is clean.
9. *faces*—Your smiling *faces* make me happy.
10. *lights*—Many bright *lights* were shining.
11. *brothers*—The two *brothers* are the same size.
12. *boxes*—Several *boxes* are on the porch.
13. *grades*—Four *grades* are in the same room.
14. *things*—Those worn-out *things* may be discarded.
15. *blocks*—The street is eight *blocks* long.
16. *these*—I think *these* papers are yours.

GRADE 4

1. *curl*—Their cat likes to *curl* up on the rug.
2. *thinner*—Mervin used the *thinner* piece of wire.
3. *saddest*—It was the *saddest* event in my life.
4. *term*—The president serves a *term* of four years.
5. *stir*—I must *stir* the pudding while it cooks.
6. *earthworm*—An *earthworm* is a round worm.
7. *newspaper*—The *newspaper* advertised a stove.
8. *busiest*—Summer is the *busiest* season for them.
9. *sir*—"Good evening, *sir*," the boy said.
10. *germs*—Some *germs* cause diseases.
11. *burnt*—The Jews gave *burnt* offerings to God.
12. *biggest*—Rabbits ate the *biggest* plants.
13. *squirrel*—The *squirrel* moved swiftly.
14. *earlier*—Eugene came *earlier* than I did.
15. *oldest*—Methuselah was the *oldest* person.
16. *all right*—Donald is *all right* again.

Many in the *world* have a *birthday* today.
We must *hurry* to get to market *early*.

GRADE 7

1. *specified*—Mother *specified* the length of drapes.
2. *possibility*—There is a *possibility* of failure.
3. *affected*—Naaman was *affected* by leprosy.
4. *sensible*—Bodies need a *sensible* amount of rest.
5. *affectionate*—Frisky is an *affectionate* puppy.
6. *development*—The housing *development* was built.
7. *cooperate*—You must *cooperate* with the dentist.
8. *effective*—Is this an *effective* fly spray?
9. *comfortable*—Our home is small but *comfortable*.
10. *facility*—Is there a cooking *facility* in the park?
11. *artificial*—My cousin has an *artificial* leg.
12. *operation*—Addition is an *operation* in math.
13. *factories*—We visited two glass *factories*.
14. *available*—How much space is *available* to us?
15. *favorably*—Did he respond *favorably* to our invitation?
16. *perfectly*—A sphere is *perfectly* round.
17. *believable*—This story hardly sounds *believable*.
18. *feasible*—Your answer seems *feasible* to me.
19. *fashionable*—The Bible forbids *fashionable* clothing.
20. *beneficial*—Sunshine is *beneficial* to our health.
21. *miserable*—Satan is a *miserable* taskmaster.
22. *production*—Egg *production* is slowly increasing.
23. *certificate*—He needed a *certificate* of identification.
24. *professor*—Mr. Brown is a college *professor*.
25. *changeable*—What is more *changeable* than wind?

GRADE 8

1. *photograph*—I have a *photograph* of Great-grandfather.
2. *residence*—It shows the *residence* where he lived.
3. *remembrance*—A picture is a special *remembrance*.
4. *ascension*—That was before their *ascension* to the hill farm.
5. *decorations*—Donna did the *decorations* on the cake.
6. *leisurely*—A *leisurely* walk refreshed us.
7. *brilliancy*—The *brilliancy* of the stars was glorious!
8. *constellation*—Do you know the *constellation* above Orion?
9. *intelligence*—Man's *intelligence* is puny.
10. *microphone*—The *microphone* stopped working.
11. *audience*—Half the *audience* could not hear.
12. *amuse*—A mean joke does not *amuse* a gentleman.
13. *illuminate*—God can *illuminate* the darkest heart.
14. *hatred*—He changed Saul's *hatred* to love.
15. *resistance*—Saul's program of *resistance* stopped.
16. *allegiance*—He switched his *allegiance* to Christ.
17. *iniquities*—All his *iniquities* were washed away.
18. *ceased*—Persecution *ceased* in Jerusalem.
19. *correspondence*—The girls' *correspondence* was inspiring.
20. *evidently*—They were *evidently* good friends.
21. *violence*—Someone threatened *violence* on the plane.
22. *emergency*—The pilot made an *emergency* landing.
23. *auditor*—The records are ready for the *auditor*.
24. *efficient*—We appreciate *efficient* bookkeeping.
25. *discrepancy*—A small *discrepancy* appeared in the figures.

LESSON 15

GRADE 2

1. *started*—We have *started* to take a test.
2. *worked*—Noah *worked* hard to build the ark.
3. *talked*—Jesus *talked* to the woman at the well.
4. *helped*—The Israelite maid *helped* Naaman's wife.
5. *hunted*—The shepherd *hunted* for the lost sheep.
6. *washed*—The blind man *washed* in the pool of Siloam.
7. *stayed*—Samuel *stayed* to help Eli.
8. *missed*—Mary and Joseph *missed* Jesus.
9. *turned*—They *turned* back to Jerusalem.
10. *snowed*—After it *snowed* the ground was white.
11. *rained*—How much has it *rained* since yesterday?
12. *played*—The children *played* quiet games.

GRADE 5

1. *compare*—A customer likes to *compare* prices.
2. *prepare*—It is time to *prepare* for church.
3. *farther*—He went *farther* than I did.
4. *sincerely*—We *sincerely* desire to do good.
5. *warehouse*—A big *warehouse* is behind the shop.
6. *appear*—New buds will *appear* in the spring.
7. *queer*—The duck made a *queer* noise.
8. *smart*—The *smart* fox stayed away from the trap.
9. *repair*—The kind boy offered to *repair* her bike.
10. *therefore*—Wayne was sick; *therefore* he went to bed.
11. *careless*—The *careless* lad broke his toy.
12. *hardware*—That man owns a *hardware* store.
13. *departure*—The boy's *departure* was unnoticed.
14. *Holy Spirit*—The *Holy Spirit* is one of the Trinity.
15. *dearest*—Jesus is our *dearest* friend.
16. *hero*—David became *hero* when he killed Goliath.

My *parents* needed gas *sooner*.

The *lowest* part of your *heart* points to the left.

GRADE 6

1. *international*—This is an *international* airport.
2. *instructor*—The flight *instructor* is here.
3. *observation*—We stood on the *observation* deck.
4. *reference*—He brought a *reference* book.
5. *regularly*—The planes are inspected *regularly*.
6. *tailor*—This suit was made by a *tailor*.
7. *embroidery*—That is good *embroidery* work.
8. *deliveries*—There will not be many *deliveries* today.
9. *failure*—There was a power *failure* yesterday.
10. *debtor*—The *debtor* could not pay what he owed.
11. *permission*—Do you have *permission* to leave?
12. *reverence*—Always show *reverence* in church.
13. *ignorant*—Jonathan was *ignorant* of Saul's command.
14. *governor*—He is the *governor* of our state.
15. *miners*—The coal *miners* work hard.
16. *scholarship*—His work shows good *scholarship*.

Show the *customer* a *battery*.

These *factories* make *oyster* crackers.

GRADE 3

1. *planted*—The men *planted* trees beside the road.
2. *ended*—When recess *ended*, we came indoors.
3. *selling*—The farmer is *selling* his extra corn.
4. *packed*—Have you *packed* your suitcase?
5. *cooked*—Mother has *cooked* the potatoes for dinner.
6. *standing*—Someone was *standing* in the doorway.
7. *bringing*—The postman is *bringing* our mail.
8. *crying*—The baby has stopped *crying* now.
9. *jumped*—Frogs *jumped* into the water.
10. *buying*—What are we *buying* at the store?
11. *blowing*—The wind was *blowing* all day.
12. *cleaned*—Have you *cleaned* your room?
13. *filled*—The widow *filled* all the vessels.
14. *pray*—We always *pray* before we eat lunch.
15. *boxes*—Both *boxes* are empty.
16. *gifts*—The wise men gave *gifts* to Jesus.

GRADE 4

1. *parents*—Harold's *parents* love to sing.
2. *somewhere*—God buried Moses *somewhere* in a valley.
3. *everywhere*—Snow lay *everywhere* outdoors.
4. *grandpa*—We plan to visit our *grandpa* soon.
5. *heart*—A person's *heart* is the size of his fist.
6. *prayer*—We end every *prayer* with "amen."
7. *wears*—Mother *wears* a covering.
8. *truly*—We are *truly* blessed by God.
9. *friendly*—We must be *friendly* to have friends.
10. *their*—The children recited *their* poems.
11. *fairly*—Games played *fairly* are enjoyable.
12. *slowly*—A car came *slowly* in the lane.
13. *tear*—A *tear* slid down her cheek.
14. *grandfather*—His *grandfather* has gray hair.
15. *sharp*—Carry a *sharp* knife with the point down.
16. *nearly*—The sun shone *nearly* all day.
    I *ate* my share of the *deer* meat.
    A *pair* of new boots may *cheer* the poor man.

GRADE 7

1. *detract*—Sloppy writing will *detract* from the message.
2. *acknowledge*—Everyone should *acknowledge* God.
3. *essential*—Fuel is *essential* to a fire.
4. *repulsive*—Lukewarmness is *repulsive* to God.
5. *actually*—The larger dog was *actually* younger.
6. *spiritual*—God's Word is our *spiritual* bread.
7. *historical*—The city has great *historical* value.
8. *subtrahend*—The *subtrahend* is smaller than the minuend.
9. *approval*—Your father's *approval* is important.
10. *impelling*—An inner force was *impelling* Lynn to go on.
11. *technical*—Engineering requires *technical* skill.
12. *attraction*—Niagara Falls is a known *attraction*.
13. *impulsive*—Foolish, *impulsive* buyers lose money.
14. *controlled*—The weather is *controlled* by God.
15. *compel*—God does not *compel* anyone to serve Him.
16. *knight*—Long ago, a *knight* lived in a castle.
17. *dispatch*—Did the king *dispatch* a messenger?
18. *contractor*—The *contractor* gave us an estimate.
19. *personal*—Our *personal* appearance tells about us.
20. *ordinance*—Jesus taught the *ordinance* of Feet Washing.
21. *criminal*—The guilty *criminal* was sentenced.
22. *repellent*—This mosquito *repellent* works well.
23. *parallel*—Many streets have *parallel* parking.
24. *crystal*—Put the flowers into a *crystal* vase.
25. *contracts*—A muscle *contracts* when we use it.

GRADE 8

1. *satellite*—The moon is a *satellite* of the earth.
2. *meteorite*—Could this odd pebble be a *meteorite?*
3. *calorie*—Figure the *calorie* content of that dessert.
4. *contrite*—God honors a *contrite* spirit.
5. *infinite*—His *infinite* view sees the heart.
6. *behavior*—We see the fruits of *behavior.*
7. *faithfully*—Let us serve Him *faithfully.*
8. *thermostat*—The *thermostat* was bumped to 85 degrees.
9. *dedicate*—We could *dedicate* our recess to cleaning.
10. *nonsense*—Goliath's threat was no *nonsense.*
11. *armor*—David rejected the *armor* of Saul.
12. *challenge*—His *challenge* angered the giant.
13. *surplus*—David had four *surplus* stones.
14. *Israelite*—The *Israelite* army sprang to action.
15. *favorite*—That is Eric's *favorite* Bible story.
16. *indefinite*—We can use an *indefinite* number of volunteers.
17. *convenient*—Choose a *convenient* spot to meet.
18. *appetite*—Larry has a big *appetite* after school.
19. *refrigerator*—It often leads him to the *refrigerator.*
20. *beggar*—We met a *beggar* on the street corner.
21. *regretting*—He was *regretting* his choice.
22. *buyer*—Along came a *buyer* for his labor.
23. *exceedingly*—He was *exceedingly* grateful for the work.
24. *thermometer*—The *thermometer* showed a record cold.
25. *surgeon*—The *surgeon* was as relieved as anyone.

LESSON 16

GRADE 2

1. *telling*—I heard Mother *telling* him to wait.
2. *falling*—Nuts are *falling* from the tree.
3. *putting*—Is Gloria *putting* the groceries away?
4. *waiting*—He is probably tired of *waiting* for me.
5. *reading*—We are *reading* an interesting story.
6. *singing*—The birds were *singing* since daybreak.
7. *snowing*—When it is *snowing*, we wear boots.
8. *fishing*—We saw men *fishing* through the ice.
9. *doing*—The boys are *doing* their work.
10. *running*—The motor is *running* quietly.
11. *sending*—Mother is *sending* two letters today.
12. *saying*—The man was *saying* something about fish.

GRADE 5

1. *metal*—That *metal* post is bent.
2. *final*—Study for the *final* test.
3. *finally*—A decision was *finally* made.
4. *awful*—The burnt potatoes had an *awful* smell.
5. *carefully*—The girl *carefully* did her lessons.
6. *capitol*—They drove past the *capitol* building.
7. *formal*—His *formal* ways are interesting.
8. *national*—Route 30 is a *national* road.
9. *settled*—They are *settled* in their new house.
10. *nickel*—How much will a *nickel* buy?
11. *restless*—The boy was *restless* all night.
12. *tremble*—Sinners will *tremble* before God.
13. *devil*—The *devil* tempted Eve in the garden.
14. *faithful*—Paul was *faithful* until death.
15. *central*—Love is the *central* theme of 1 John.
16. *Gospel*—Paul preached the *Gospel* of salvation.
    We hunted the lost *buckle* in the *capital* city.
    Can you spell *angel* and *ankle* right?

GRADE 6

1. *approach*—We could not *approach* the horse.
2. *adventure*—They had an *adventure* today.
3. *channel*—The *channel* looks deep.
4. *manufacturing*—This is a *manufacturing* state.
5. *Scripture*—The *Scripture* is God's Word.
6. *butcher*—Father worked in a *butcher* shop.
7. *stretch*—It is refreshing to *stretch*.
8. *dispatch*—Will you *dispatch* this message?
9. *charity*—Show *charity* to all.
10. *cheerful*—He sang a *cheerful* song.
11. *fortunate*—That is a *fortunate* man.
12. *moisture*—The *moisture* on the grass soon dried up.
13. *natural*—Jesus used *natural* illustrations.
14. *disappear*—How could it *disappear* so quickly?
15. *disappointed*—I was *disappointed* in the book.
16. *independence*—United States won *independence* in 1783.
    The *Christian* trusts in his *Redeemer*.
    The *engineer* had to make a *choice*.

GRADE 3

1. *lighted*—The room is *lighted* by three windows.
2. *staying*—Is anyone *staying* at home?
3. *saved*—God *saved* Noah in the ark.
4. *hoped*—Zacchaeus *hoped* to see Jesus.
5. *coming*—The people were *coming* closer.
6. *living*—Rahab was *living* in Jericho.
7. *loved*—Jesus *loved* Mary, Martha, and Lazarus.
8. *used*—Why have you *used* that color?
9. *having*—We are *having* guests for dinner.
10. *giving*—The sun is *giving* light all the time.
11. *making*—Nancy was *making* sandwiches for lunch.
12. *lived*—Who had *lived* in that house?
13. *moving*—The earth is *moving* around the sun.
14. *pile*—A *pile* of books is on the desk.
15. *cleaned*—The windows were *cleaned* on Saturday.
16. *buying*—Mother is *buying* groceries.

GRADE 4

1. *temple*—A Christian's body is the *temple* of God.
2. *needle*—Did you find Aunt Mary's *needle* for her?
3. *buckle*—Carl helped Philip to *buckle* his boots.
4. *travel*—I hope to *travel* to another state.
5. *gentle*—Our pony is a *gentle* animal.
6. *healthy*—Thank God for a *healthy* body.
7. *turtle*—A box *turtle* can make a good pet.
8. *angry*—Do not be *angry* with others.
9. *animals*—Many *animals* went into the ark.
10. *rainy*—We have had much *rainy* weather.
11. *evil*—Every person is born with an *evil* nature.
12. *bottle*—The milk *bottle* is nearly empty.
13. *muddy*—The hurricane left *muddy* water everywhere.
14. *marbles*—The *marbles* rolled across the floor.
15. *angel*—God sent an *angel* to help Daniel.
16. *idol*—Aaron disobeyed and made an *idol* of gold.
   Handle the *pencil* with care.
   Who put *dirty* marks in the *middle* of the hall?

GRADE 7

1. *immigrant*—Carlos was an *immigrant* from Mexico.
2. *bankruptcy*—The business filed for *bankruptcy*.
3. *excellent*—Mrs. Yoder is an *excellent* seamstress.
4. *liable*—Which party was *liable* for the accident?
5. *continuous*—Loving others is a *continuous* debt.
6. *obligation*—Our first *obligation* is to obey God.
7. *ligament*—A torn *ligament* can be very painful.
8. *absolutely*—The cave was *absolutely* dark.
9. *exorbitant*—Farms sold for *exorbitant* prices.
10. *assistant*—The teacher's *assistant* checked our papers.
11. *solution*—Seawater is a *solution* of salt.
12. *maintenance*—Ask the *maintenance* man to fix it.
13. *correspondent*—He is a newspaper *correspondent*.
14. *resolve*—Daniel's firm *resolve* kept him from sin.
15. *interrupt*—It is impolite to *interrupt* others.
16. *dissolve*—Sugar can *dissolve* in water.
17. *league*—The Gibeonites desired a *league* with Israel.
18. *requirements*—The state's *requirements* are for our good.
19. *impatient*—The *impatient* horse pawed the ground.
20. *contradiction*—"I did not!" is a *contradiction*.
21. *obtained*—Enoch *obtained* favor with God.
22. *erupt*—When will that volcano *erupt* again?
23. *intelligent*—Man is an *intelligent* being.
24. *ceiling*—Our kitchen *ceiling* has been lowered.
25. *indicate*—Orange signs *indicate* road construction.

GRADE 8

1. *appendicitis*—Carol had *appendicitis* last month.
2. *arthritis*—Grandfather suffers from *arthritis*.
3. *prescribe*—What did the doctor *prescribe* for pain?
4. *competent*—We are glad for *competent* doctors.
5. *anointing*—The sick may call for *anointing* with oil.
6. *authority*—God has final *authority* on healing.
7. *conferred*—Three men *conferred* about the damage.
8. *abstract*—The wallpaper has an *abstract* pattern.
9. *Sabbath*—The *Sabbath* ended at sundown.
10. *delinquent*—A *delinquent* payment damaged his credit.
11. *transcribe*—Can you *transcribe* the message on tape?
12. *additional*—We need four *additional* copies.
13. *civilized*—Most people in a *civilized* culture can read.
14. *literature*—It is important to choose good *literature*.
15. *literary*—What are your *literary* interests?
16. *subscription*—Renew your *subscription* before it expires.
17. *bored*—Children get *bored* if they play all the time.
18. *autograph*—Harlan let his friends *autograph* his cast.
19. *exceptional*—Dr. Mason did *exceptional* lettering.
20. *manuscript*—Joel used tall *manuscript* characters.
21. *telegraph*—News of the disaster came by *telegraph*.
22. *photograph*—A large *photograph* was on the front page.
23. *esteemed*—Saints have always *esteemed* the psalms highly.
24. *deeply*—Drink *deeply* of their inspiration.
25. *enlighten*—God will *enlighten* your understanding.

LESSON 17

GRADE 2

1. *wood*—Cherry *wood* makes pretty furniture.
2. *began*—Suddenly the rain *began* to fall.
3. *wagon*—James fixed the *wagon* wheel.
4. *eating*—The cows are *eating* hay.
5. *hung*—We *hung* the pictures on the wall.
6. *father*—Jesse was the *father* of David.
7. *Jesus*—Cruel men hung *Jesus* on the cross.
8. *Amen*—We say *Amen* at the end of our prayers.
9. *mother*—Hannah was the *mother* of Samuel.
10. *any*—Was there *any* food left?
11. *after*—The boy ran *after* the ball.
12. *list*—We made a *list* of all the names.

GRADE 5

1. *return*—You may *return* the book.
2. *unable*—An infant is *unable* to walk.
3. *rotten*—The apple was *rotten* at the core.
4. *unknown*—For some *unknown* reason, he left.
5. *commandment*—They obeyed the *commandment* willingly.
6. *certainly*—He *certainly* is a happy boy.
7. *carbon*—Here is a sheet of *carbon* paper.
8. *margin*—Keep your *margin* straight.
9. *invitation*—This *invitation* is for you.
10. *knock*—Did you hear a *knock* on the door?
11. *American*—Some *American* Indians lived in wigwams.
12. *invention*—His wonderful *invention* didn't work.
13. *knot*—My shoelace has a *knot* in it.
14. *Christian*—There have been many *Christian* martyrs.
15. *Canaan*—The land of *Canaan* is west of the Jordan.
16. *renew*—Waiting on God will *renew* our strength.

   Ask God *often* for *wisdom*.

   The boys asked the man a *common question*.

GRADE 6

1. *insurance*—Carefulness is good *insurance* against accidents.
2. *assure*—Let me *assure* you that you are correct.
3. *machinery*—The *machinery* was very noisy.
4. *patience*—Have *patience* till he comes.
5. *delicious*—That was a *delicious* meal.
6. *appreciate*—We *appreciate* your help.
7. *especially*—The night seemed *especially* cold.
8. *congregation*—The *congregation* knelt to pray.
9. *stationery*—I took *stationery* along to write letters.
10. *stationary*—He crashed into a *stationary* vehicle.
11. *situation*—This *situation* is not good.
12. *combination*—The *combination* to the safe is lost.
13. *definition*—What is the *definition* of this word?
14. *fashion*—The *fashion* of the world will perish.
15. *generation*—This is the *generation* of them that seek Thee.
16. *publish*—Can you *publish* this book?

   We gave *shelter* to the *anxious* man.

   The *penmanship* on this *invitation* is beautiful.

GRADE 3

1. *again*—Jesus will come *again* to the earth.
2. *only*—The widow had *only* a pot of oil.
3. *eaten*—The people had not *eaten* all the food.
4. *thumb*—Hold your *thumb* over the hole.
5. *eggs*—Twelve *eggs* fill one carton.
6. *sweep*—Remember to *sweep* the floor.
7. *basket*—He wants the *basket* with the handle.
8. *colors*—Seven *colors* are in the rainbow.
9. *hate*—We should *hate* sin.
10. *strange*—The motor made a *strange* noise.
11. *tiger*—The *tiger* is a large cat.
12. *pencil*—Is your *pencil* sharp?
13. *taking*—The sick child is *taking* medicine.
14. *lights*—Bright *lights* shone on the bridge.
15. *giving*—What are you *giving* as a gift?
16. *moving*—The hands on the clock are *moving* slowly.

GRADE 4

1. *robin*—In the spring the *robin* flies north.
2. *ocean*—The waters of the *ocean* never stop moving.
3. *lessons*—The Bible has many *lessons* for us.
4. *eighteen*—We will buy *eighteen* oranges.
5. *ninety*—Not many people live *ninety* years.
6. *ribbon*—The Jews wore a blue *ribbon* on their garments.
7. *person*—One other *person* works there.
8. *nineteen*—Rebecca is *nineteen* years old.
9. *seventeen*—Ernest has *seventeen* rabbits.
10. *fifth*—What did God make on the *fifth* day?
11. *cousin*—My aunt and my *cousin* made cookies.
12. *eighty*—Did you read *eighty* pages?
13. *happened*—The accident *happened* around noon.
14. *thirteen*—Uncle Abram milks *thirteen* cows.
15. *often*—We thank our parents *often* for their care.
16. *fifteenth*—It suits on the *fifteenth* of May.

Mary made *cotton* dresses for her *seven* girls.

Had he wanted *thirty* or *sixty* chairs?

GRADE 7

1. *conquer*—Satan will never *conquer* the church.
2. *librarian*—Ask the *librarian* to reserve the book.
3. *antecedent*—Thinking right is *antecedent* to doing right.
4. *pressure*—Water *pressure* increases with depth.
5. *curious*—After our accident, *curious* people came.
6. *seize*—The border police will *seize* illegal goods.
7. *appetite*—Many people have no *appetite* for olives.
8. *congress*—A country's *congress* can pass new laws.
9. *extension*—We asked for an *extension* of time.
10. *application*—Nelson filled out an *application*.
11. *reflected*—Titus's image was *reflected* in the water.
12. *complexion*—A Jew has a dark *complexion*.
13. *applied*—Barbara *applied* oil to the squeaky hinges.
14. *flexible*—A garden hose is *flexible* and soft.
15. *expression*—The king saw Nehemiah's *expression*.
16. *attendant*—The station *attendant* checked our oil.
17. *guardian*—Mordecai was Esther's *guardian*.
18. *auxiliary*—"Will" is an *auxiliary* verb.
19. *inflection*—Our voice *inflection* helps to show our meaning.
20. *reflexes*—Your muscle *reflexes* are automatic.
21. *complicated*—Digestion of food is a *complicated* process.
22. *intention*—His *intention* was not to deny Christ.
23. *republican*—America has a *republican* government.
24. *compressor*—The air *compressor* would not work.
25. *tongue*—An anteater's *tongue* is long and thin.

GRADE 8

1. *tuberculosis*—Is *tuberculosis* very serious?
2. *diphtheria*—It is not as critical as *diphtheria*.
3. *diagnosis*—We heard the *diagnosis* on Anthony today.
4. *measles*—He has *measles* the second time.
5. *epidemic*—Could there be an *epidemic?*
6. *hypnotic*—Some doctors use *hypnotic* methods.
7. *melancholy*—Did that cause his *melancholy* moods?
8. *label*—Read the *label* carefully.
9. *helicopter*—The tail rotor keeps a *helicopter* from spinning.
10. *drowned*—Heavy rains *drowned* our first planting of peas.
11. *all right*—The later crop looks *all right*.
12. *convey*—A small ditch will *convey* irrigation water.
13. *metropolis*—Joel moved away from the *metropolis*.
14. *population*—The *population* increased rapidly.
15. *suburb*—Soon his country village was a *suburb* of the city.
16. *democracy*—God does not rule the church by *democracy*.
17. *politician*—Every *politician* protects his reputation.
18. *civilian*—The president wears *civilian* clothes.
19. *interval*—Can you sing the musical *interval* correctly?
20. *atone*—Jesus came to *atone* for all man's sin.
21. *possession*—He gives the priceless *possession* of peace.
22. *humility*—Christ's *humility* is a pattern for us.
23. *suspicious*—It pays to be *suspicious* of your own pride.
24. *icicles*—A row of *icicles* sparkled in the sun.
25. *inconvenience*—Service does not measure *inconvenience*.

LESSON 18

*See Teacher's Manual for special instructions.

GRADE 2

1. *boys*—May we *boys* have the swings?
2. *girls*—Three *girls* walked past the house.
3. *trees*—Pine *trees* bear pine cones.
4. *birds*—Two *birds* built a nest above the door.
5. *rooms*—The *rooms* in their house are big.
6. *nights*—In winter the *nights* seem long.
7. *bushes*—Look under the *bushes* for the kittens.
8. *houses*—All the *houses* looked alike.
9. *babies*—Several *babies* cried at once.
10. *cows*—At milking time the *cows* walked to the barn.
11. *turned*—Father *turned* the steering wheel.
12. *started*—Suddenly the wind *started* to blow.
13. *worked*—The ants had *worked* hard to build the tunnel.
14. *washed*—Have you *washed* your hands?
15. *helped*—The boys *helped* Father paint the fence.
16. *singing*—Everyone was *singing* happily.
17. *waiting*—The sheep are *waiting* to be sheared.
18. *falling*—I heard something *falling* to the floor.
19. *doing*—What are you *doing* now?
20. *running*—Why is he *running* so fast?
21. *Jesus*—An angel told the shepherds that *Jesus* was born.
22. *mother*—Samuel's *mother* made him a coat.
23. *father*—"Honour thy *father* and thy mother."
24. *after*—The visitors went home *after* dinner.
25. *wagon*—The tractor pulled the *wagon* to the field.

GRADE 5

1. *return*—Some day Jesus will *return* to the earth.
2. *unable*—I was *unable* to take the lid off.
3. *smart*—My dog is *smart* enough to trail rabbits.
4. *renew*—You may *renew* your book at the library.
5. *hero*—David is a *hero* in the Bible.
6. *farther*—Go no *farther* than the bridge.
7. *windy*—A *windy* day makes me tired.
8. *group*—Read the next *group* of words.
9 *repair*—Nehemiah wanted to *repair* the city walls.
10. *careless*—The *careless* girl made more work for her mother.
11. *whom*—To *whom* did Nancy give cookies?
12. *worse*—The storm is *worse* today than yesterday.
13. *curtain*—The rain came down like a *curtain*.
14. *worried*—I *worried* that we would be late.
15. *view*—What a lovely *view* you have of the river.
16. *devil*—Satan is the *devil* who deceived Eve.
17. *Gospel*—The *Gospel* is good news for everybody.
18. *Canaan*—The land of *Canaan* was given to Abram.
19. *carbon*—I will make a *carbon* copy for you.
20. *invention*—The *invention* of engines changed people's lives.
21. *unknown*—That name is *unknown* to me.
22. *sermon*—The *sermon* was on John 11.
23. *margin*—Keep the left-hand *margin* straight.
24. *avenue*—Many houses were built along the *avenue*.
25. *beauty*—Look at the *beauty* all around you.

GRADE 6

1. *grieve*—"Do not *grieve* for me," Jesus said.
2. *league*—A *league* is an ancient measure of distance.
3. *depot*—The bus *depot* was crowded.
4. *veil*—Moses wore a *veil* over his face.
5. *ceiling*—Does the *ceiling* need to be painted?
6. *cedar*—Hiram sent *cedar* to Solomon.
7. *unbeliever*—Do not argue with an *unbeliever*.
8. *children's*—The *children's* boots are muddy.
9. *relief*—It is a *relief* to hear your voice.
10. *medium*—The color was *medium* brown.
11. *circulation*—Grandpa has poor *circulation*.
12. *burden*—The minister has a *burden* for his people.
13. *missionary*—The *missionary* came home.
14. *courtesy*—He had the *courtesy* to apologize.
15. *firmament*—God created the *firmament*.
16. *eternal*—We can trust God's *eternal* promises.
17. *furnace*—The *furnace* heated the house.
18. *merchant*—Is that a *merchant* ship?
19. *research*—You have done your *research* well.
20. *observation*—We watched from the *observation* deck.
21. *deliveries*—Our grocer makes *deliveries*.
22. *reserve*—The *reserve* has wild geese.
23. *scholarship*—This essay shows good *scholarship*.
24. *regularly*—We *regularly* pray before meals.
25. *tailor*—Is there a *tailor* in this town?

GRADE 3

1. *thinks*—A good student *thinks* hard.
2. *path*—"Follow the *path* of Jesus."
3. *thine*—We pray "For *thine* is the kingdom."
4. *teacher's*—This is the *teacher's* desk.
5. *father's*—Here is my *father's* shop.
6. *covers*—The *covers* of the book are loose.
7. *sisters*—How many *sisters* do you have?
8. *bones*—The *bones* are for the dog.
9. *ashes*—Mordecai sat in *ashes* and mourned.
10. *boxes*—Bring the *boxes* with books in them.
11. *packed*—Mother *packed* my lunch.
12. *jumped*—The children *jumped* rope.
13. *ended*—The story *ended* at a good place.
14. *buying*—Father is *buying* some cows.
15. *crying*—The baby was *crying* loudly.
16. *saved*—Jerry wisely *saved* his money.
17. *loved*—Jesus always has *loved* children.
18. *lived*—Jesus *lived* in Nazareth.
19. *making*—Are you *making* a kite?
20. *thumb*—A sore *thumb* is very troublesome.
21. *hate*—Love the good and *hate* the evil.
22. *pencil*—Is your *pencil* sharp enough?
23. *basket*—The *basket* was filled with bread.
24. *eaten*—Everyone had *eaten* and was full.
25. *again*—We will sing *again* today.

GRADE 4

1. *later*—Sooner or *later* it will rain again.
2. *schoolhouse*—The *schoolhouse* was warm.
3. *few*—"The harvest truly is great, but the labourers are *few*."
4. *sir*—I'm sorry, *sir,* but Father is not here.
5. *nearly*—Your lunch boxes are *nearly* alike.
6. *sooner*—Should we start *sooner* than two o'clock?
7. *person*—The first *person* God created was Adam.
8. *often*—Thank God *often* for a sound mind.
9. *largest*—Asia is the *largest* continent.
10. *tune*—I thought the *tune* sounded familiar.
11. *highway*—Bartimaeus sat by the *highway* begging.
12. *earthworm*—A robin ate the *earthworm* quickly.
13. *newspaper*—Put the *newspaper* on the pile.
14. *everywhere*—Weeds grew *everywhere* we looked.
15. *marbles*—Two *marbles* rolled under the sofa.
16. *animals*—God created all the *animals*.
17. *eighty*—Mother picked *eighty* quarts of berries.
18. *travel*—Wild geese *travel* many miles.
19. *muddy*—Wipe off your *muddy* shoes.
20. *smooth*—Naaman's new flesh was soft and *smooth*.
21. *temple*—The *temple* was a place of worship.
22. *saddest*—The dog had the *saddest*-looking eyes.
23. *burnt*—Forest fires have *burnt* many trees.
24. *ninety*—Who is over *ninety* years old?
25. *seventeen*—Joseph was *seventeen* when he was sold.

GRADE 7

1. *marvelous*—What a *marvelous* day!
2. *promotion*—Fred's *promotion* soon came.
3. *activity*—A hummingbird's *activity* is fascinating.
4. *thorough*—The diary was *thorough*.
5. *mischievous*—Monkeys are *mischievous* animals.
6. *agency*—We hear through the *agency* of sound waves.
7. *mobile*—An elaborate *mobile* hung from the ceiling.
8. *virtuous*—Hezekiah was a *virtuous* king.
9. *agitate*—Be careful not to *agitate* the bees.
10. *movement*—The sun's *movement* seems slow.
11. *changeable*—A chameleon has *changeable* color.
12. *affectionate*—She gave me an *affectionate* pat.
13. *effective*—Paul's ministry was *effective*.
14. *artificial*—The punch had *artificial* coloring.
15. *facility*—Elmer has great *facility* in woodcarving.
16. *believable*—A good story must seem *believable*.
17. *operation*—This machine's *operation* takes skill.
18. *sensible*—Be sure answers are *sensible*.
19. *beneficial*—Walking is a *beneficial* exercise.
20. *perfectly*—Is that sphere *perfectly* round?
21. *essential*—Food gives us *essential* vitamins.
22. *approval*—Father nodded in *approval* of our plan.
23. *subtrahend*—In 5 – 3 = 2, the *subtrahend* is 3.
24. *personal*—We should show a *personal* interest.
25. *attraction*—Explain its *attraction* to iron.

GRADE 8

1. *cosmic*—The meteor shower was caused by *cosmic* dust.
2. *heroic*—Many early Christians were *heroic* martyrs.
3. *assurance*—Strong *assurance* shone in their lives.
4. *apostolic*—Were people braver in *apostolic* times?
5. *noticeable*—True character is *noticeable* in any age.
6. *crisis*—It is especially clear in times of *crisis*.
7. *colonel*—A stern *colonel* interviewed the boys.
8. *acknowledgment*—He gave no *acknowledgment* of God.
9. *cardiac*—Could you help someone with *cardiac* problems.
10. *athletic*—An *athletic* lifestyle helps maintain a sound heart.
11. *evidently*—Stress and worry *evidently* bring health risks.
12. *ceased*—The winds *ceased* early in the morning.
13. *violence*—Broken trees revealed the *violence* of the storm.
14. *efficient*—We had an *efficient* cleanup crew.
15. *amuse*—The birds at the feeder *amuse* Grandfather.
16. *leisurely*—He adjusted well to a *leisurely* life.
17. *correspondence*—Letters are one type of *correspondence*.
18. *intelligence*—Instinct, not *intelligence*, guides animals.
19. *discrepancy*—Nancy found a *discrepancy* in the price list.
20. *allegiance*—Your uniform declares your *allegiance*.
21. *armor*—Put on the whole *armor* of God.
22. *nonsense*—There is no *nonsense* about a fire drill.
23. *thermometer*—Does the *thermometer* register accurately?
24. *surgeon*—A *surgeon* needs a steady hand.
25. *convenient*—Tell the truth even when it is not *convenient*.

LESSON 18
CONTINUED

*See Teacher's Manual for special instructions.

GRADE 5

26. *knock*—I heard a *knock* on the door.
27. *circle*—Everyone stood in a *circle* for the game.
28. *stern*—A *stern* voice said, "Keep off the grass."
29. *fuel*—Add more *fuel* to the fire.
30. *warehouse*—They loaded furniture from the *warehouse*.
31. *worst*—That was the *worst* cold I ever had.
32. *worship*—We go to church to *worship* God.
33. *tremble*—Did the windows *tremble* during the storm?
34. *therefore*—It snowed; *therefore* we couldn't go.
35. *purse*—How many pennies are in your *purse* today?
36. *compare*—We need to *compare* ourselves with the Bible.
37. *metal*—Is every kind of *metal* attracted to a magnet?
38. *commandment*—The first *commandment* is to honor God.
39. *appear*—A snake might *appear* at any time.
40. *capitol*—The dome on the *capitol* is huge.
41. *Holy Spirit*—God sent the *Holy Spirit* to the Gentiles also.
42. *earliest*—James came the *earliest* of the three workers.
43. *certainly*—We *certainly* appreciate their kindness.
44. *invitation*—I received an *invitation* to the meal.
45. *finally*—The big day *finally* came.
46. *Christian*—A *Christian* home is a blessing.
47. *Titus*—Paul wrote a letter to *Titus*.
48. *Hebrews*—The faith chapter is *Hebrews* 11.
49. *Matt.**—The first book of the New Testament is *Matthew*.
50. *Rom.**—The Book of *Romans* has sixteen chapters.

GRADE 6

26. *failure*—There was a power *failure* last night.
27. *ignorant*—Sometimes we are *ignorant* of God's blessings.
28. *permission*—Sue has *permission* to leave.
29. *governor*—The *governor* was in town today.
30. *reverence*—Samuel showed *reverence* to God.
31. *channel*—The river *channel* is deep.
32. *natural*—Trees are a *natural* resource.
33. *adventure*—We had quite an *adventure* today.
34. *cheerful*—A *cheerful* smile is like a medicine.
35. *stretch*—Do not *stretch* the truth.
36. *fortunate*—They were *fortunate* to have heat.
37. *charity*—*Charity* is the love of God.
38. *disappointed*—I was *disappointed* not to go.
39. *moisture*—Fog is one form of *moisture* in the air.
40. *independence*—Panama gained *independence* in 1903.
41. *insurance*—The widow had no *insurance*.
42. *situation*—This *situation* is getting out of hand.
43. *delicious*—Mother serves *delicious* meals.
44. *machinery*—The *machinery* ran smoothly.
45. *publish*—Let us *publish* the Gospel to all.
46. *patience*—Your *patience* is appreciated.
47. *fashion*—Judy will *fashion* her clay into a cup.
48. *definition*—Which *definition* is correct?
49. *stationary*—A *stationary* object is not moving.
50. *appreciate*—I *appreciate* your help.

GRADE 4

26. *mule*—The *mule* likes grass and oats.
27. *grandpa*—Ask your *grandpa* which he wants.
28. *fairly*—This book is *fairly* new.
29. *ocean*—The ship crossed the *ocean* in five days.
30. *lowest*—We could reach the two *lowest* branches.
31. *lessons*—I finished my *lessons* early.
32. *their*—Our neighbors lost *their* dog.
33. *heart*—God knows the secrets of each *heart*.
34. *goose*—A *goose* has webbed feet.
35. *wears*—Grandpa *wears* glasses only to read.
36. *all right*—That is *all right* with me.
37. *parents*—"Obey your *parents* in the Lord."
38. *evil*—"Deliver us from *evil*," we pray.
39. *prayer*—God heard the *prayer* of the widow.
40. *through*—Jonah walked *through* Nineveh, preaching.
41. *needle*—Can you thread the *needle* yourself?
42. *cousin*—He has no *cousin* near his age.
43. *healthy*—Working outdoors is *healthy* exercise.
44. *fifteenth*—They came on the *fifteenth* of May.
45. *term*—The school *term* is half over.
46. *squirrel*—Now the *squirrel* can eat his nuts.
47. *earlier*—If he knocked *earlier,* I did not hear.
48. *idol*—How sad to pray to an *idol* for rain.
49. *busiest*—Friday is the *busiest* day of the week.
50. *thinner*—Onionskin paper is *thinner* than this.

GRADE 7

26. *spiritual*—Christians fight a *spiritual* battle.
27. *compel*—Jesus will not *compel* anyone to serve Him.
28. *impulsive*—You may regret an *impulsive* decision.
29. *repellent*—Philip dusted the cows with *repellent*.
30. *contracts*—Father signed two building *contracts*.
31. *maintenance*—A *maintenance* man fixed a window.
32. *absolutely*—God deals *absolutely* impartially.
33. *interrupt*—An alarm clock can *interrupt* dreams.
34. *resolve*—Ruth made an earnest *resolve* to do better.
35. *assistant*—The *assistant* pilot used the controls.
36. *liable*—The top-heavy wagon seemed *liable* to topple.
37. *obligation*—His *obligation* was to care for Mary.
38. *continuous*—The earth's rotation is *continuous*.
39. *obtained*—We *obtained* a wheelchair for Grandma.
40. *excellent*—Alligators are *excellent* swimmers.
41. *application*—Put an *application* of salve on it.
42. *curious*—On our walk, *curious* cows stared at us.
43. *pressure*—Mother uses a *pressure* cooker for meat.
44. *auxiliary*—They need an *auxiliary* heating system.
45. *extension*—We had a telephone *extension* upstairs.
46. *seize*—A drowning man will *seize* anything in sight.
47. *compressor*—The air *compressor* hose broke.
48. *flexible*—This job has *flexible* working hours.
49. *intention*—My *intention* was to write to you soon.
50. *reflected*—Vernon *reflected* over the past year.

GRADE 8

26. *behavior*—Tony's *behavior* confirms his testimony.
27. *calorie*—Like a snowflake, just one *calorie* hardly counts.
28. *satellite*—The mosquito attended me like a *satellite*.
29. *indefinite*—I'll lend the book for an *indefinite* time.
30. *contrite*—God dwells with the *contrite* heart.
31. *autograph*—Boone carved his *autograph* on the door.
32. *bored*—He *bored* three holes to peg the leather hinge.
33. *literature*—Sue found some new *literature* about pioneers.
34. *exceptional*—She has *exceptional* interest in history.
35. *appendicitis*—Are there home remedies for *appendicitis*?
36. *conferred*—We *conferred* a pompous name on the rooster.
37. *subscription*—Be sure to renew your *subscription* in time.
38. *arthritis*—Uncle Roy's *arthritis* makes him our weather man.
39. *competent*—His *competent* service is free.
40. *delinquent*—The *delinquent* assignment was finally done.
41. *civilian*—Police officers sometimes dress in *civilian* clothes.
42. *suspicious*—Strange noises made us *suspicious* of visitors.
43. *diagnosis*—The final *diagnosis* was squirrel activity.
44. *convey*—What else would *convey* acorns to the attic?
45. *atone*—This gift is to *atone* for my forgetfulness.
46. *interval*—There was a long *interval* between appointments.
47. *helicopter*—The *helicopter* picked up shipwreck victims.
48. *drowned*—Some of the crew *drowned* while helping others.
49. *politician*—A clever *politician* glamorized the rescue.
50. *label*—He wanted to *label* the event for his credit.

LESSON 19

GRADE 2

1. *away*—The robin flew *away* from its nest.
2. *meal*—Breakfast is the first *meal* of the day.
3. *table*—Come to the *table* for breakfast.
4. *may*—Yes, you *may* gather the eggs.
5. *gate*—Open the *gate* for the cattle.
6. *key*—Turn the *key* to open the lock.
7. *mail*—The mailman brings our *mail* to us.
8. *free*—Our neighbors gave away *free* puppies.
9. *asleep*—Jesus was *asleep* in the boat.
10. *afraid*—The disciples were *afraid* in the storm.
11. *money*—How much *money* does it cost?
12. *leaf*—A sassafras *leaf* sometimes looks like a mitten.

GRADE 5

1. *Joel*—The name *Joel* means "Jehovah is God."
2. *Amos*—The prophet *Amos* was a shepherd.
3. *Jonah*—God called *Jonah* to Nineveh.
4. *Micah*—The man *Micah* was a prophet.
5. *altar*—The *altar* was made of stones.
6. *Creator*—God is the *Creator* of the universe.
7. *favorite*—What is your *favorite* color?
8. *quiet*—Be very *quiet* in the hospital.
9. *famous*—Fannie Crosby was a *famous* poet.
10. *area*—In what *area* do you live?
11. *furniture*—Dust all the *furniture* in the room.
12. *mineral*—Coal is a *mineral* found in the earth.
13. *separate*—We must *separate* the egg yolks and whites.
14. *president's*—We respect the *president's* authority.
15. *acres*—He farms fifty *acres* of land.
16. *salute*—Friends *salute* each other with a greeting.
    Father bought *groceries* and other *supplies* in town.
    Our *teacher's* family are all *Mennonites*.

GRADE 6

1. *pier*—The *pier* was covered with water.
2. *irrigate*—We must *irrigate* this field.
3. *miracles*—Jesus did many *miracles* there.
4. *sincere*—We must be *sincere* and honest.
5. *heretofore*—Nothing *heretofore* had been like this.
6. *materials*—The building *materials* have arrived.
7. *preparing*—I am *preparing* dinner.
8. *swear*—Do not *swear* at all.
9. *aware*—I am *aware* of that.
10. *heir*—Isaac was *heir* to Abraham.
11. *affair*—The whole *affair* was a misunderstanding.
12. *radar*—The pilot watched his *radar* screen.
13. *guard*—We must *guard* against lying.
14. *garbage*—Put the *garbage* in the bag.
15. *who'd*—There was no one *who'd* seen it.
16. *who'll*—Can you find someone *who'll* go?
    On the *contrary*, we *weren't* late at all.
    He *appeared* to *declare* the truth.

GRADE 3

1. *planning*—What are you *planning* to do?
2. *getting*—We will be *getting* new pencils.
3. *cutting*—The children are *cutting* out pictures.
4. *gotten*—Has anyone *gotten* the mail?
5. *setting*—You may begin *setting* the table.
6. *sitting*—Grandfather is *sitting* in his chair.
7. *stopped*—The donkey *stopped* and would go no farther.
8. *waited*—The ten virgins *waited* for the bridegroom.
9. *letting*—Father is *letting* the engine run.
10. *handed*—The customer *handed* the money to the clerk.
11. *swimming*—Beavers are *swimming* in the water.
12. *added*—Our neighbors *added* two rooms to their house.
13. *turning*—I heard the key *turning* in the lock.
14. *thumb*—A sore *thumb* can hinder good handwriting.
15. *step*—The bottom *step* looks dirty.
16. *tag*—Children play *tag* sometimes.

GRADE 4

1. *preacher*—Noah was a *preacher* of righteousness.
2. *supply*—"But my God shall *supply* all your need."
3. *company*—Jesus fed a great *company* of people.
4. *enemy*—Our *enemy* Satan wants us to do bad things.
5. *Trinity*—In the *Trinity* there are three persons.
6. *Mennonite*—The *Mennonite* people obeyed God.
7. *among*—Divide the apples *among* the three girls.
8. *surprise*—Did the sun *surprise* you?
9. *balloon*—A toy *balloon* stretches.
10. *different*—A wasp is *different* from a bee.
11. *interesting*—How *interesting* to watch ants!
12. *sugar*—Much *sugar* comes from sugar cane.
13. *holiday*—A Thanksgiving *holiday* is once a year.
14. *arithmetic*—In *arithmetic* we add numbers.
15. *grandma's*—Amy saw her *grandma's* old chest.
16. *teacher's*—The *teacher's* helpers are cleaning.

The *driver* loads boxes of many *colors*.
One *thousand* jars were in the *cellar*.

GRADE 7

1. *edition*—This is the third *edition* of our paper.
2. *explanation*—Please give an *explanation* to me.
3. *exhibit*—We enjoyed the museum's airplane *exhibit*.
4. *dependent*—A baby is totally *dependent* on others.
5. *experiment*—We will *experiment* with bean seeds.
6. *existing*—Only a few bald eagles are *existing* now.
7. *compensation*—Ray received *compensation* for his work.
8. *expenditure*—Buying a car is a big *expenditure*.
9. *premium*—Do you buy *premium* gasoline?
10. *effort*—With *effort*, Lois pulled the stubborn weed.
11. *credible*—He had a *credible* reason for being late.
12. *exemption*—The blind receive a tax *exemption*.
13. *expose*—Do not *expose* yourself to unsound teaching.
14. *enrolled*—Twenty children *enrolled* in the class.
15. *eliminate*—We must try to *eliminate* bad habits.
16. *expenses*—His employer paid his business *expenses*.
17. *enormous*—Whales are *enormous* mammals.
18. *redemption*—Our *redemption* was bought by Jesus.
19. *extremely*—Dynamite is *extremely* dangerous.
20. *estate*—A deceased person's *estate* belongs to his heirs.
21. *excellent*—Moses was an *excellent* leader.
22. *exaggerated*—Goliath *exaggerated* his strength.
23. *honestly*—The apostle Paul lived *honestly* before men.
24. *excommunicate*—Churches *excommunicate* sinful members.
25. *virtuous*—Dorcas was a *virtuous* woman.

GRADE 8

1. *Exodus*—Moses is the main character in *Exodus*.
2. *occurred*—Signs and wonders *occurred* before Pharaoh.
3. *surrender*—He had many chances to *surrender* to God.
4. *extraordinary*—His army came to an *extraordinary* end.
5. *incense*—Israel's praise was a sweet *incense* to God.
6. *dissatisfied*—The people were *dissatisfied* with manna.
7. *carbohydrates*—*Carbohydrates* provide fuel for the body.
8. *energy*—Sugar is a fast *energy* food.
9. *courier*—A faithful *courier* will be prompt.
10. *discourse*—His *discourse* was short but meaningful.
11. *emphasis*—The main *emphasis* was on safety.
12. *ordinary*—Expression makes an *ordinary* story special.
13. *eclipse*—A lunar *eclipse* happens only at full moon.
14. *excursion*—We enjoyed an *excursion* to the creek.
15. *encounter*—Sam expected to *encounter* a snake.
16. *exclaim*—We heard him *exclaim* something to Noah.
17. *embroider*—Use blue floss to *embroider* the bird.
18. *example*—John is a good *example* of steadfastness.
19. *exile*—He did not waste his time in *exile*.
20. *endure*—Those who *endure* will be saved.
21. *ascend*—Many prayers *ascend* for strength.
22. *anticipate*—We *anticipate* great joy in heaven.
23. *transcend*—It will *transcend* any earthly pleasure.
24. *installation*—Are you ready for *installation* as captain?
25. *encourage*—Let us *encourage* one another.

LESSON 20

GRADE 2

1. *boat*—A small *boat* sailed on the water.
2. *ago*—Long *ago* people had no telephones.
3. *find*—Try to *find* the answer yourself.
4. *cold*—If I am *cold*, I wear a sweater.
5. *buy*—Mother will *buy* groceries.
6. *light*—A bright *light* shone in the dark.
7. *own*—Does each one have his *own* book?
8. *by*—A yellow cat sat *by* the door.
9. *fight*—Those birds *fight* too much.
10. *blow*—The wind might *blow* our papers.
11. *over*—The calf jumped *over* the fence.
12. *eye*—His right *eye* became blind.

GRADE 5

1. *torn*—Her dress is *torn* just a little.
2. *thought*—He *thought* it was empty.
3. *awoke*—The fire siren *awoke* us.
4. *toward*—The owl glided *toward* the mouse.
5. *officers*—Both *officers* asked us questions.
6. *drawn*—The picture was *drawn* freehand.
7. *sisters*—How many *sisters* do you have?
8. *visitors*—Give *visitors* a warm welcome.
9. *mourn*—They *mourn* the loss of their kitten.
10. *neighbors*—Our *neighbors* are friendly.
11. *horror*—A look of *horror* crossed her face.
12. *sister's*—What is your oldest *sister's* name?
13. *tore*—She *tore* the rag in half.
14. *Almighty*—Our God is the *Almighty*.
15. *fought*—David *fought* the Philistines.
16. *daughter*—Dinah was the *daughter* of Jacob.
    He painted the *fourth* barn last *autumn*.
    Have you *caught* those fish and *brought* them along?

GRADE 6

1. *overalls*—These *overalls* are dirty.
2. *abroad*—He was *abroad* for a month.
3. *lawyer*—A *lawyer* wanted to tempt Jesus.
4. *dawn*—The *dawn* of the day is here.
5. *laundry*—Take the *laundry* outside.
6. *author*—Christ is the *author* of eternal salvation.
7. *faucet*—The *faucet* is leaking.
8. *ore*—The iron *ore* was melted down.
9. *mortal*—We are *mortal* creatures.
10. *ordain*—The church will *ordain* a minister.
11. *source*—Christ is the *source* of living water.
12. *quarrel*—Abraham would not *quarrel* with Lot.
13. *glorify*—Christ came to *glorify* the Father.
14. *how's*—But *how's* that going to work?
15. *what's*—I wonder *what's* in this box.
16. *where's*—Now *where's* my screwdriver?
    Was there *moss* in the old *orchard*?
    He had an *automatic* right to the *territory*.

GRADE 3

1. *thousand*—Jesus fed five *thousand* people.
2. *bow*—Mordecai would not *bow* to Haman.
3. *joy*—Living for Jesus brings *joy* and peace.
4. *spoil*—Too much salt will *spoil* the cake.
5. *flower*—That red *flower* is a tulip.
6. *plow*—The tractor pulled a *plow* through the field.
7. *south*—Some birds fly *south* for the winter.
8. *flour*—Sift two cups of *flour* into the bowl.
9. *sounds*—That noise *sounds* familiar.
10. *join*—In cursive writing we *join* the letters.
11. *oil*—Father put a quart of *oil* into the engine.
12. *round*—Pour the cake batter into *round* pans.
13. *owl*—We heard the *owl* hooting at bedtime.
14. *stopped*—A policeman *stopped* all the traffic.
15. *waited*—The people *waited* to cross the street.
16. *sitting*—Who is *sitting* next to the window?

GRADE 4

1. *glory*—"The *glory* gates are ever open wide."
2. *because*—"We love him, *because* he first loved us."
3. *brought*—Sick people were *brought* to Jesus.
4. *adore*—"O come, let us *adore* Him!"
5. *enemies*—"Love your *enemies*," Jesus said.
6. *forty*—God sent rain for *forty* days.
7. *friends*—Job's *friends* did not speak at first.
8. *friend's*—Her *friend's* house is made of adobe.
9. *farmer's*—A ladybug is a *farmer's* friend.
10. *farmers*—Many *farmers* live in Central America.
11. *caught*—The men *caught* the latex in a cup.
12. *smaller*—A wren is *smaller* than a robin.
13. *orange*—The pack rat took the *orange* button.
14. *seesaw*—A *seesaw* is also called a teeter-totter.
15. *naughty*—We put the *naughty* puppy outside.
16. *chalkboard*—Is our *chalkboard* a blackboard?

Why do you put *straw* on the *lawn*?

That *cloth costs* two dollars.

GRADE 7

1. *deferred*—We *deferred* our trip until next year.
2. *reduction*—A discount is a *reduction* in price.
3. *substitute*—Margarine is a *substitute* for butter.
4. *collateral*—Mr. Hansen used his car as *collateral* for a loan.
5. *agitate*—Bubbles form when we *agitate* soapy water.
6. *denomination*—Which *denomination* do we attend?
7. *relation*—Nancy is a blood *relation* of mine.
8. *consequently*—Anna fell and *consequently* broke her leg.
9. *inspect*—We wanted to *inspect* the pretty butterfly.
10. *difference*—Tell the *difference* between the two.
11. *sequence*—Number them in the proper *sequence*.
12. *covenant*—God made a *covenant* with Abraham.
13. *educational*—A visit to the zoo is *educational*.
14. *transferred*—Brian *transferred* to our school.
15. *declaration*—They rejected his *declaration* of truth.
16. *executive*—A business *executive* makes many decisions.
17. *submitted*—Jesus *submitted* to His Father's will.
18. *deduct*—Did you *deduct* any points from his score?
19. *latitude*—Lines of *latitude* encircle a globe.
20. *subway*—The Millers rode a *subway* in the city.
21. *deference*—We must show *deference* to the elderly.
22. *mobile*—A new *mobile* home was being set up.
23. *doctrine*—The Sadducees taught a false *doctrine*.
24. *persecution*—Paul suffered severe *persecution*.
25. *despise*—God does not *despise* a humble heart.

GRADE 8

1. *warrior*—Paul was a *warrior* for Christ.
2. *epistles*—His *epistles* give practical guidance.
3. *borne*—The eaglet was *borne* to safety by its mother.
4. *environment*—They soared above a stormy *environment*.
5. *epidermis*—Oil makes the *epidermis* waterproof.
6. *insomnia*—Two nights of *insomnia* weakened Sue's health.
7. *pneumonia*—Is that why she took *pneumonia*?
8. *epilepsy*—Medicines can control *epilepsy* to a degree.
9. *nineteenth*—The Civil War was in the *nineteenth* century.
10. *epidemic*—Save the field trip till the *epidemic* is past.
11. *threaten*—We do not want to *threaten* the health of others.
12. *refreshment*—Singing brings *refreshment* to weary souls.
13. *chord*—A beautiful *chord* is repeated throughout the song.
14. *abundance*—There is an *abundance* of corn in the freezer.
15. *recommend*—Do you *recommend* that we plant more?
16. *previous*—Think of ways to use the *previous* supply.
17. *algebra*—The thought patterns of *algebra* are very logical.
18. *vague*—Study the rules that are *vague* in your memory.
19. *summon*—Try to *summon* your best skills for the test.
20. *quotations*—Carefully punctuate all *quotations*.
21. *psychology*—The music in stores utilizes *psychology*.
22. *schedule*—Our *schedule* permits several reports.
23. *oblige*—You will *oblige* us by reading clearly.
24. *amusing*—It is *amusing* to compare impressions.
25. *ridiculous*—You need not answer a *ridiculous* question.

LESSON 21

GRADE 2

1. *took*—Mother *took* the bread from the oven.
2. *food*—The *food* in our lunches is delicious.
3. *pushed*—Larry *pushed* the box into the corner.
4. *cook*—We will *cook* potatoes for dinner.
5. *moon*—The *moon* gets its light from the sun.
6. *shoe*—Can you tie your *shoe* yourself?
7. *Jew*—Queen Esther was a *Jew*.
8. *looked*—Jesus *looked* up to heaven and prayed.
9. *who*—Do you know *who* climbed a tree to see Jesus?
10. *full*—The bottle is *full* of milk.
11. *shoot*—This plant is sending out a new *shoot*.
12. *you*—A letter came for *you* in the mail.

*See Teacher's Manual for special instructions.

GRADE 5

1. *goodness*—Thank God for His *goodness* to us.
2. *treasure*—Our wonderful *treasure* is the Bible.
3. *pure*—Keep your heart *pure* and holy.
4. *sparrow*—God sees even a *sparrow* fall.
5. *ladies*—Four *ladies* worked at a quilt.
6. *lady's*—One *lady's* glasses broke.
7. *understood*—He *understood* Spanish well.
8. *shook*—We *shook* hands with the older folks.
9. *worn*—He felt *worn* out from the busy day.
10. *pulpit*—The minister's *pulpit* was made of oak.
11. *tour*—We took a *tour* through the factory.
12. *cure*—Penicillin helps to *cure* diseases.
13. *members*—Two family *members* are missing.
14. *pleasure*—It is a *pleasure* to read neat writing.
15. *usual*—When is your *usual* bedtime.
16. *written*—Whose name is *written* at the bottom?
    The *woman* looked for *sugar* in the big store.
    No yellow *chicks* were asleep *during* the storm.

GRADE 6

1. *mature*—A *mature* person is not quickly offended.
2. *bulletin*—We rearranged the *bulletin* board.
3. *jewel*—A valuable *jewel* was stolen.
4. *bruise*—There was a *bruise* under his eye.
5. *Jerusalem*—Jesus went to *Jerusalem* often.
6. *influence*—Do not let evil men *influence* you.
7. *assured*—He *assured* me that he was all right.
8. *procured*—Two disciples *procured* a colt for Jesus.
9. *reducing*—Are you *reducing* your fractions?
10. *produced*—The fields have *produced* abundantly.
11. *including*—Many people, *including* Jacob, went to Egypt.
12. *admitted*—David *admitted* that he had sinned.
13. *preferred*—Daniel was *preferred* above other rulers.
14. *propeller*—The plane's *propeller* has stopped.
15. *develop*—A bad cold can *develop* into pneumonia.
16. *attempt*—Do not *attempt* to do that alone.
    He *introduced* an idea that few people *believed*.
    The captain *approved* the plan without *losing* any time.

GRADE 3

1. *lawn*—Rain makes the *lawn* turn green.
2. *straw*—Some farmers wear *straw* hats.
3. *costs*—Do not buy it if it *costs* too much.
4. *cloth*—Spread a clean *cloth* on the table.
5. *also*—A rabbit can *also* be called a bunny.
6. *already*—Have you *already* done your chores?
7. *strong*—Samson was a *strong* man.
8. *always*—Jesus *always* obeyed Mary and Joseph.
9. *walked*—The people *walked* to Jerusalem.
10. *belongs*—That pencil *belongs* to me.
11. *bought*—Customers *bought* the homemade bread.
12. *drawing*—Someone is *drawing* a good picture.
13. *along*—May I go *along* with you?
14. *sounds*—The wheel *sounds* as if it needs oil.
15. *join*—First *join* hands to form a circle.
16. *owl*—A screech *owl* lived in the woods.

GRADE 4

1. *cookies*—Mother made *cookies* yesterday.
2. *should*—Pencil lead *should* be called graphite.
3. *wool*—A sheep's *wool* is sheared once a year.
4. *pudding*—We gave our *pudding* to the travelers.
5. *during*—Woodchucks hibernate *during* the winter.
6. *fully*—A *fully* grown hummingbird is quite small.
7. *wouldn't*—Plants *wouldn't* grow without light.
8. *couldn't*—I *couldn't* read the Braille message.
9. *you're*—No, *you're* not to eat the leaves.
10. *haven't*—The word *haven't* is a contraction.
11. *pulled*—Men *pulled* Jeremiah up from the dungeon.
12. *woman*—Jesus asked the *woman* for a drink.
13. *inch**—I placed the picture an *inch* from the edge.
14. *foot**—We planted the flowers a *foot* apart.
15. *yard**—A *yard* is a little shorter than a meter.
16. *mile**—The Mount of Olives is about a *mile* long.

Could a *wolf* eat a goose?

Your brother *stood* among the bushes.

GRADE 7

1. *contrition*—Psalm 51 shows David's *contrition*.
2. *diverse*—The world has many *diverse* languages.
3. *conversation*—The boys' *conversation* was about tractors.
4. *caution*—Handle explosives with great *caution*.
5. *conversion*—Saul's *conversion* was near Damascus.
6. *involved*—Our church is *involved* in a prison work.
7. *circuit*—Electricity travels in a *circuit*.
8. *converted*—He *converted* our oil furnace to gas.
9. *revolution*—The moon's *revolution* takes a month.
10. *circumference*—We measured its *circumference*.
11. *conviction*—Brother John talked with *conviction*.
12. *rhubarb*—Mother baked a *rhubarb* pie.
13. *circumstances*—Under no *circumstances* should we steal.
14. *cooperation*—This job requires *cooperation*.
15. *wrought*—The railing was made of *wrought* iron.
16. *coarse*—Cornmeal is a *coarse* flour.
17. *circular*—The earth travels in a *circular* path.
18. *visual*—Our eyes are *visual* organs.
19. *communication*—Prayer is *communication*.
20. *essential*—Water is *essential* to living things.
21. *possibility*—There is a *possibility* I may come.
22. *compliance*—We want willing *compliance* with the rules.
23. *wrestle*—Ralph found it hard to *wrestle* with the problem.
24. *coordinate*—Which will *coordinate* with yellow?
25. *confirming*—His honesty is *confirming* our trust.

GRADE 8

1. *parables*—Jesus often spoke in *parables*.
2. *instruction*—His *instruction* was for all who would hear.
3. *frequently*—Everyday stories *frequently* hold spiritual truth.
4. *precious*—These truths are very *precious*.
5. *paradise*—The pardoned thief gained *paradise* that day.
6. *acceptable*—His faith was *acceptable* to God.
7. *paralyze*—A broken back could *paralyze* you.
8. *contemplate*—Seriously *contemplate* safety measures.
9. *inspection*—Give careful *inspection* to work areas.
10. *sensible*—A *sensible* approach will prevent many accidents.
11. *periodical*—Have a *periodical* review of safety rules.
12. *philosophy*—"Work before play" is a good *philosophy*.
13. *Philemon*—Paul's letter to *Philemon* came from Rome.
14. *persuade*—He wrote to *persuade* him to receive Onesimus.
15. *dealt*—As a Christian he surely *dealt* kindly with his slave.
16. *angel*—An *angel* appeared to Gideon.
17. *urgent*—There was an *urgent* need for a leader.
18. *recognized*—Gideon *recognized* God's plan.
19. *hastily*—He *hastily* instructed his soldiers.
20. *accompanied*—Twelve disciples *accompanied* Jesus.
21. *perimeter*—Conrad mowed the *perimeter* of the lawn first.
22. *sophomore*—Are you ready for *sophomore* studies?
23. *parachute*—The skydiver had a huge red *parachute*.
24. *conspicuous*—It made a *conspicuous* show in the sunshine.
25. *parasite*—The deer tick is an obnoxious *parasite*.

LESSON 22

GRADE 2

1. *helps*—Sunshine *helps* plants to grow.
2. *begins*—Spring *begins* here in March.
3. *goes*—The robin *goes* north for the summer.
4. *likes*—No one *likes* to hear people complain.
5. *gets*—The early bird *gets* the worm.
6. *sees*—Our cat hides when she *sees* visitors.
7. *needs*—Every *needs* oxygen to breathe.
8. *plays*—That big fish *plays* in the water.
9. *takes*—Grandfather *takes* two pills every day.
10. *lives*—A Frenchman *lives* in France.
11. *stands*—A statue *stands* in the harbor.
12. *turns*—The little wheel *turns* the big wheel.

*See Teacher's Manual for special instructions.

GRADE 5

1. *powder*—Sift the baking *powder* with the flour.
2. *usually*—When do you *usually* brush your teeth?
3. *doubt*—I *doubt* that he heard me.
4. *destroy*—Fires *destroy* many things.
5. *loyal*—The servant was *loyal* to his master.
6. *surely*—The sunset *surely* was beautiful.
7. *safety*—Our *safety* is in the Lord.
8. *silence*—Sirens pierced the *silence* of the night.
9. *lonely*—The old house looked *lonely* and sad.
10. *booklet*—The cover of the *booklet* is torn.
11. *towel*—Hang a clean *towel* on the rod.
12. *coward*—The dog was a *coward* and ran away.
13. *route*—What *route* do you travel to go there?
14. *wound*—Unkind words can *wound* a person's feelings.
15. *boiler*—A *boiler* gives off much steam.
16. *traveler*—The tired *traveler* stopped to rest.

   She was *collecting* snow water as it *melted*.
   My *voice* should always be *friendly* and kind.

GRADE 6

1. *division*—These problems in *division* are not hard.
2. *garage*—The *garage* should be cleaned out.
3. *measure*—Did you *measure* that correctly?
4. *encounter*—Jacob had an *encounter* with God.
5. *announce*—An angel came to *announce* Jesus' birth.
6. *bough*—Absalom was caught by the *bough* of an oak.
7. *devout*—Simeon was a *devout* man.
8. *foul*—The river had a *foul* smell.
9. *fowl*—A creature that has feathers is a *fowl*.
10. *nowadays*—Smallpox is not a threat *nowadays*.
11. *account*—Every man must someday give *account* to God.
12. *bound*—Samson was *bound* and taken away.
13. *driven*—The car was *driven* a thousand miles.
14. *shone*—The sun *shone* brightly.
15. *sought*—The shepherd *sought* his lost sheep.
16. *stole*—"Let him that *stole* steal no more."

   People do not *usually* *drown* in shallow water.
   I *doubt* that you can *pronounce* all Hebrew words.

GRADE 3

1. *porch*—Sweep the *porch* before Grandmother comes.
2. *cord*—Plug the *cord* into the outlet.
3. *morning*—How early in the *morning* will you go?
4. *shore*—Along the *shore* lay beautiful seashells.
5. *four*—A square has *four* corners.
6. *before*—Think *before* you speak.
7. *deer*—A young *deer* is a fawn.
8. *ears*—The dog perked up his *ears* and ran.
9. *years*—Is David three or four *years* old?
10. *cheer*—A bouquet of flowers will *cheer* the lady.
11. *sort*—Grandmother wants me to *sort* her buttons.
12. *fork*—Lay the *fork* to the left of the plate.
13. *Lord*—"The *Lord* is my shepherd."
14. *strong*—Around Jericho was a *strong* wall.
15. *always*—"Men ought *always* to pray."
16. *also*—"We ought *also* to love one another."

GRADE 4

1. *points*—A compass needle always *points* north.
2. *counter*—The kitchen *counter* is cracked.
3. *enjoying*—The boys are *enjoying* the ride.
4. *mouth*—A delta forms at the *mouth* of a river.
5. *cannot*—We *cannot* do wrong and feel right.
6. *boy's*—The new *boy's* name is Andrew.
7. *joined*—We *joined* them in singing.
8. *wasn't*—Alaska *wasn't* a state until 1959.
9. *aren't*—Why *aren't* you able to locate Greenland?
10. *won't*—We *won't* be able to see Mount Mitchell.
11. *crowd*—In the *crowd* was a woman who needed Jesus.
12. *ground*—Saul fell to the *ground* and prayed.
13. *hour**—"I need Thee ev'ry *hour,* / Most gracious Lord."
14. *week**—The first day of the *week,* Jesus arose.
15. *month**—For *month,* the Indian said moon.
16. *year**—For over a *year,* Ezekiel lay on his side.

John will buy *flour* and a *plow.*
Why did you *spoil* that pretty *flower?*

GRADE 7

1. *interfere*—The weather could *interfere* with our plans.
2. *remittance*—Please send your *remittance* soon.
3. *succeed*—Joash could not *succeed* without God.
4. *convention*—This *convention* is held every year.
5. *interior*—The trailer's *interior* walls were brown.
6. *enterprise*—His new business *enterprise* failed.
7. *dismissal*—Before *dismissal,* they sang a song.
8. *missionary*—Lucy is a *missionary* in Africa.
9. *internal*—Our heart is an *internal* organ.
10. *exceed*—Drivers should not *exceed* the speed limit.
11. *admission*—The museum's *admission* charge is low.
12. *illustrate*—Many parables *illustrate* truth.
13. *successfully*—They *successfully* completed their work.
14. *hygiene*—Daily *hygiene* includes brushing our teeth.
15. *inspired*—The Bible was *inspired* by God.
16. *committee*—The food *committee* planned the dinner.
17. *reindeer*—Herds of *reindeer* live in Lapland.
18. *investigate*—The police will *investigate* the burglary.
19. *succession*—He fired three shots in *succession.*
20. *conceit*—God despises *conceit* and flattery.
21. *precede*—Plowing must *precede* sowing.
22. *intercede*—Jesus will *intercede* with God for us.
23. *convenience*—Enclose an envelope for his *convenience.*
24. *relieve*—Drugs are used to *relieve* pain.
25. *seize*—An angry crowd tried to *seize* Jesus.

GRADE 8

1. *geometry*—Surveyors use *geometry* in their work.
2. *language*—Mary's second *language* is Swedish.
3. *flannel*—We can use this *flannel* for shirts.
4. *visible*—It has a barely *visible* flaw.
5. *satisfactory*—The price is very *satisfactory.*
6. *dehydrate*—This drier will *dehydrate* any kind of fruit.
7. *hydrogen*—Use *hydrogen* peroxide to prevent infection.
8. *peasant*—An ordinary *peasant* could read the Bible.
9. *individual*—Baptism was by *individual* choice.
10. *Anabaptist*—The *Anabaptist* way was severely persecuted.
11. *beaten*—Many were *beaten,* burned, or drowned.
12. *privilege*—It was a *privilege* to suffer for Christ.
13. *physical*—They were willing to lose *physical* life.
14. *passage*—Death was their *passage* to heaven.
15. *convenient*—A protractor is a *convenient* tool.
16. *anatomy*—Alligator *anatomy* is similar to the crocodile's.
17. *assessment*—Tax *assessment* was raised last year.
18. *hydraulic*—Keep *hydraulic* hoses in good repair.
19. *hydrant*—Water gushed out of the *hydrant.*
20. *occasional*—We like an *occasional* change.
21. *musician*—King David was a skilled *musician.*
22. *commerce*—Solomon had *commerce* with many lands.
23. *magnificent*—Tourists came for the *magnificent* scenery.
24. *analysis*—Rangers made an *analysis* of their visits.
25. *crusade*—They launched a *crusade* for cleaner parks.

LESSON 23

1. *were*—Many butterflies *were* in the air.
2. *herself*—She *herself* wrote the poem.
3. *never*—In heaven people will *never* be sick.
4. *pearl*—The beautiful *pearl* was inside the shell.
5. *paper*—Tear the *paper* neatly from the tablet.
6. *yesterday*—The day before today we call *yesterday*.
7. *learn*—We like to *learn* Bible verses.
8. *words*—Try to spell all the *words* correctly.
9. *burn*—The priests needed to *burn* sacrifices.
10. *under*—Abraham's visitors rested *under* the tree.
11. *first*—Genesis is the *first* book in the Bible.
12. *working*—Matthew was *working* when Jesus called him.

*See Teacher's Manual for special instructions.

GRADE 5

1. *judge*—Which *judge* in Israel was a woman?
2. *soldier*—Paul was a brave *soldier* of Christ.
3. *rejoice*—We will *rejoice* in the Lord.
4. *destroyed*—Sin has always *destroyed* peace.
5. *religion*—We are thankful for freedom of *religion*.
6. *generally*—When do you *generally* eat supper?
7. *engineer*—The *engineer* blew his whistle.
8. *shortage*—A *shortage* of rain affects crops.
9. *pledge*—Both nations will *pledge* to help each other.
10. *allowed*—He was *allowed* to go out.
11. *object*—The garden was the *object* of discussion.
12. *student*—Every *student* worked quietly.
13. *gem*—A child is a *gem* in the sight of God.
14. *postage*—I remember *postage* being only five cents.
15. *drown*—A car engine will *drown* out in deep water.
16. *Judah*—The Southern Kingdom was called *Judah*.
   The nurse *stepped* into a small, *disorderly* room.
   Look at these *beautiful* clouds after I *dismiss* school.

GRADE 6

1. *adjustment*—Make an *adjustment* on this chair.
2. *hedge*—The Lord keeps a *hedge* around His people.
3. *hygiene*—Good *hygiene* helps to keep us healthy.
4. *percentage*—A large *percentage* of the crop was destroyed.
5. *baggage*—He left his *baggage* on the train.
6. *journey*—That was a long *journey* for you.
7. *jury*—Most criminals receive a *jury* trial.
8. *injury*—He suffered not one *injury* in the accident.
9. *heroes*—Hebrews 11 lists many *heroes* of the faith.
10. *buffalo*—The *buffalo* belongs to the cattle family.
11. *scissors*—Have you seen my *scissors* today?
12. *series*—We had a *series* of meetings last week.
13. *gentlemen*—Show these *gentlemen* to their room.
14. *salesman*—We had a *salesman* at the house.
15. *basis*—On what *basis* do you judge him?
16. *pajamas*—Put the *pajamas* in the drawer.
   You were *generous* to *suggest* it.
   Did the *pigeon* go along on the *voyage?*

GRADE 3

1. *bark*—Some dogs *bark* at strangers.
2. *farm*—Boys enjoy feeding *farm* animals.
3. *starting*—The rain is *starting* to fall.
4. *scare*—Loud noises *scare* the fish.
5. *share*—I will *share* the songbook with you.
6. *chairs*—Are there enough *chairs* for everyone?
7. *marked*—The man *marked* where the posts should be.
8. *gardens*—Beautiful *gardens* are not full of weeds.
9. *bear*—The *bear* crawled into his den.
10. *care*—Someone should *care* for the flowers.
11. *pair*—Here is a new *pair* of mittens.
12. *air*—Cool *air* blew across our faces.
13. *ark*—Noah built the *ark* as God said.
14. *years*—The king was only eight *years* old.
15. *four*—Say the first *four* New Testament books.
16. *before*—Hebrews comes *before* James.

GRADE 4

1. *I'll*—The people sang, "*I'll* live for Him."
2. *didn't*—The woman *didn't* find it difficult.
3. *doesn't*—Why *doesn't* it stay warm all year?
4. *that's*—The woman said, "Why, *that's* my coin!"
5. *giant*—David was not afraid of the *giant* Goliath.
6. *charge*—Did the publican *charge* too much money?
7. *bridge*—One *bridge* is twenty-eight miles long.
8. *enjoyed*—Yesterday we *enjoyed* playing outdoors.
9. *vegetables*—Some *vegetables* have long roots.
10. *edge*—The *edge* of the sword is very sharp.
11. *changed*—A dike *changed* the swamp to farmland.
12. *oranges*—Eating *oranges* gives you vitamin C.
13. *package*—Dennis delivered the *package* to her.
14. *St.**—Main *Street* crosses Mountain Road.
15. *Ave.**—Go to Third *Avenue* and turn left.
16. *Rd.**—Spring Valley *Road* runs north and south.

    Is it *strange* to make berries into *jelly*?
    That *huge stage* is all wood.

GRADE 7

1. *locality*—In which *locality* do you live?
2. *disapprove*—Christians *disapprove* of cheating.
3. *invalid*—Our class sang for an old *invalid* lady.
4. *opponent*—Larry's *opponent* won the checkers game.
5. *disposition*—Susan has a sunny *disposition*.
6. *negligent*—Lazy, *negligent* farmers reap poorly.
7. *transgressions*—Jesus forgave the woman's *transgressions*.
8. *aggressive*—Samson was *aggressive* and bold.
9. *gradually*—The joy *gradually* faded from his eyes.
10. *negotiations*—After many *negotiations*, a price was set.
11. *statute*—A common *statute* mile measures 5,280 feet.
12. *consideration*—After *consideration*, we moved.
13. *assistance*—Do you need *assistance* with this?
14. *graduate*—Soon Michael will *graduate* from school.
15. *nonresistance*—God commands *nonresistance*.
16. *unnecessary*—During class, *unnecessary* talk is forbidden.
17. *constitution*—A healthy *constitution* resists illness.
18. *impossible*—Nothing is *impossible* with God.
19. *stationery*—Anna gave pink *stationery* to Linda.
20. *deposit*—Father made a *deposit* in the bank.
21. *flexible*—Rubber is a *flexible* material.
22. *stationary*—A moving object is not *stationary*.
23. *institute*—We attended an *institute* last weekend.
24. *disagreeable*—Camels are often *disagreeable*.
25. *guardian*—Our *guardian* angels watch over us.

GRADE 8

1. *embroidery*—Elsie does very fine *embroidery*.
2. *Almighty*—The *Almighty* is a sure refuge.
3. *anxiety*—That eases all our *anxiety*.
4. *security*—This *security* is ours through Jesus.
5. *vengeance*—We leave all *vengeance* with God.
6. *curiosity*—Leon's eyes sparkled with *curiosity*.
7. *scratchy*—He heard *scratchy* noises in the trash can.
8. *theme*—Does your program have a *theme*?
9. *dreary*—A smile can change a *dreary* day.
10. *sufficient*—Everyone has *sufficient* time for politeness.
11. *maturity*—Consistent kindness is a mark of *maturity*.
12. *strict*—Keep a *strict* control on words.
13. *divinity*—Jesus' *divinity* accompanied His humanity.
14. *practical*—Take a *practical* approach to life.
15. *reality*—Hard work is a *reality* for everyone.
16. *moody*—Overcome *moody* feelings with a song.
17. *dynamic*—Brother Seth displays *dynamic* Christianity.
18. *loyalty*—All can see his *loyalty* to Christ.
19. *certainty*—He has faith in the *certainty* of God's guidance.
20. *inferiority*—Do you see the *inferiority* of reasoning to faith?
21. *necessity*—Water is a *necessity* of life.
22. *unanimous*—The plan was accepted by *unanimous* vote.
23. *tyranny*—A revolt threw off the *tyranny* of the despot.
24. *anarchy*—The people soon found that *anarchy* was worse.
25. *humidity*—Heat is less stressful when the *humidity* is low.

LESSON 24

*See Teacher's Manual for special instructions.

GRADE 2

1. *table*—Set the *table* for dinner.
2. *away*—Father went *away* today.
3. *mail*—What came in the *mail* today?
4. *leaf*—A maple *leaf* is different from an oak leaf.
5. *asleep*—The calves are *asleep* in the barn.
6. *find*—Can you *find* the leak?
7. *light*—The sun gives *light* during the day.
8. *eye*—Can you see with one *eye* closed?
9. *boat*—John sailed his little *boat* on the water.
10. *blow*—You may *blow* out the candle.
11. *you*—Mother wants *you* to work now.
12. *moon*—Some nights the *moon* shines brightly.
13. *took*—The mechanic *took* the wheel off the truck..
14. *shoe*—Please tie your left *shoe* again.
15. *full*—The dam is *full* of water now.
16. *needs*—The baker *needs* more flour.
17. *lives*—Grandmother *lives* in a small house.
18. *helps*—When everyone *helps*, the work gets done fast.
19. *sees*—Jane *sees* the train go by every day.
20. *goes*—My shadow always *goes* with me.
21. *under*—See the dog *under* the tree.
22. *first*—Adam was the *first* man.
23. *working*—Samuel was *working* in the temple.
24. *burn*—The priests needed to *burn* sacrifices.
25. *learn*—We try to *learn* Bible verses.

GRADE 5

1. *booklet*—This little *booklet* is interesting.
2. *awoke*—When I *awoke*, the sun was shining.
3. *sisters*—Both of his *sisters* are ill.
4. *torn*—That paper is *torn* at the top.
5. *thought*—No one *thought* it would rain.
6. *goodness*—"Surely *goodness* and mercy shall follow me."
7. *pure*—"Blessed are the *pure* in heart."
8. *members*—Church *members* help each other.
9. *tore*—He *tore* the paper straight.
10. *fought*—Paul said, "I have *fought* a good fight."
11. *worn*—My coat is *worn* at the elbow.
12. *understood*—Everyone *understood* the problem.
13. *pulpit*—The minister stood behind the *pulpit*.
14. *visitors*—All the *visitors* left again.
15. *object*—Which *object* would you like to use?
16. *traveler*—The weary *traveler* rested awhile.
17. *gem*—A diamond is a *gem* most beautiful.
18. *written*—Have you *written* that letter yet?
19. *daughter*—She is the mailman's *daughter*.
20. *safety*—Fasten your *safety* belts.
21. *area*—The airport covers an immense *area* of land.
22. *Almighty*—We praise the *Almighty* for His goodness.
23. *destroyed*—Fire *destroyed* the whole building.
24. *shortage*—Was there a *shortage* of sugar then?
25. *postage*—Put enough *postage* on the package.

GRADE 6

1. *pier*—From the *pier*, I can watch the boat.
2. *aware*—David was *aware* of God's presence.
3. *swear*—We must not *swear* oaths.
4. *irrigate*—The farmer plans to *irrigate* this field.
5. *radar*—*Radar* is used to check traffic speed.
6. *sincere*—Please accept my *sincere* apology.
7. *affair*—This *affair* does not concern you.
8. *who'd*—I saw the man *who'd* been sick.
9. *materials*—These *materials* are for my project.
10. *guard*—We must *guard* against envy.
11. *abroad*—The news of Christ's birth was spread *abroad*.
12. *ore*—Much copper *ore* is mined from open pits.
13. *source*—Christ is the *source* of true peace.
14. *lawyer*—A *lawyer* tried to trap Jesus.
15. *author*—God is the *author* of the Bible.
16. *glorify*—Our lives should *glorify* God.
17. *mortal*—We cannot trust in *mortal* man.
18. *what's*—Tell me *what's* wrong, and I'll help you.
19. *ordain*—The church plans to *ordain* a minister.
20. *quarrel*—Abram would not *quarrel* with Lot.
21. *mature*—She is *mature* for her age.
22. *jewel*—A *jewel* is a precious stone.
23. *bulletin*—Did you decorate the *bulletin* board?
24. *reducing*—*Reducing* cost increases profit.
25. *bruise*—These apples will *bruise* easily.

GRADE 3

1. *swimming*—See the fish *swimming* around.
2. *planning*—We are *planning* a trip.
3. *gotten*—We have *gotten* our tests.
4. *waited*—The boys *waited* a long time.
5. *turning*—We are *turning* the pages.
6. *south*—Birds fly *south* in the fall.
7. *plow*—It is time to *plow* the field.
8. *oil*—Moses used *oil* to anoint Aaron.
9. *joy*—We have *joy* when we obey.
10. *lawn*—We will mow the *lawn* today.
11. *cloth*—The blue *cloth* is for my dress.
12. *along*—I want to go *along* with Father.
13. *always*—God's Word is *always* true.
14. *bought*—Father *bought* a new Bible.
15. *porch*—We stood on the *porch* yesterday.
16. *shore*—At the *shore* we watch seagulls.
17. *four*—We saw *four* white ducks.
18. *deer*—Two *deer* ran across the road.
19. *years*—How many *years* old are you?
20. *bear*—A black *bear* was in the forest.
21. *scare*—Do bears *scare* you?
22. *share*—We kindly *share* with others.
23. *care*—Jesus does *care* for me.
24. *chairs*—We will sit on *chairs* to read.
25. *before*—We pray *before* we eat.

GRADE 4

1. *week*—The carpenter worked a *week* on the roof.
2. *year*—Next *year* will come soon enough.
3. *foot*—That is the wrong *foot* for this shoe.
4. *cannot*—Without a key, you *cannot* unlock it.
5. *hour*—We don't know what *hour* Jesus will come.
6. *pulled*—The tractor *pulled* the wagon.
7. *won't*—My pen *won't* write any more.
8. *ground*—The multitude sat on the *ground* to eat.
9. *brought*—Wise men *brought* gifts to Jesus.
10. *because*—They worshiped Him *because* He is King.
11. *farmers*—Two *farmers* are plowing.
12. *didn't*—People *didn't* always have automobiles.
13. *chalkboard*—Write on the *chalkboard* neatly.
14. *sugar*—Pass the *sugar,* please.
15. *joined*—The visitors *joined* us in singing.
16. *surprise*—Did Grandpa *surprise* you?
17. *enjoying*—The children are *enjoying* the story.
18. *package*—Hold the *package* carefully.
19. *adore*—Praise and *adore* the Lord.
20. *giant*—The *giant* Goliath was nearly nine feet tall.
21. *caught*—His kite is *caught* in a tree.
22. *crowd*—The *crowd* followed Jesus.
23. *wouldn't*—The cow *wouldn't* leave her calf.
24. *wool*—Sheep need their *wool* in winter.
25. *seesaw*—All recess the *seesaw* went up and down.

GRADE 7

1. *exhibit*—Joseph did not *exhibit* a hateful attitude.
2. *premium*—God places a *premium* on human life.
3. *dependent*—We are *dependent* on God.
4. *expenses*—Our living *expenses* increase every year.
5. *eliminate*—Does this spray *eliminate* all weeds?
6. *explanation*—What *explanation* was given?
7. *estate*—Are we content with our *estate* in life?
8. *extremely*—Our crops produced *extremely* well.
9. *exemption*—Blindness receives tax *exemption*.
10. *redemption*—Our *redemption* is by blood.
11. *deferred*—Our meeting is *deferred* until next week.
12. *collateral*—Property is *collateral* for loans.
13. *sequence*—The *sequence* was difficult to follow.
14. *substitute*—Grandmother uses a salt *substitute*.
15. *difference*—Find a *difference* between the rocks.
16. *submitted*—We *submitted* her best story.
17. *covenant*—Israel made a *covenant* with God.
18. *executive*—An *executive* decides company policies.
19. *deduct*—A bank will *deduct* a monthly service charge.
20. *persecution*—The early church had *persecution*.
21. *compliance*—His *compliance* brought peace.
22. *circuit*—The moon travels in a *circuit* each month.
23. *diverse*—Insects are a most *diverse* group.
24. *circumstances*—Her *circumstances* are poor.
25. *conversation*—The *conversation* soon ended.

GRADE 8

1. *dissatisfied*—Mother was *dissatisfied* with the garden.
2. *energy*—We all put some *energy* into weeding.
3. *anticipate*—Now we *anticipate* better production.
4. *incense*—Prayer is a sweet *incense* to God.
5. *emphasis*—There should be more *emphasis* on sacrifice.
6. *excursion*—Absalom's *excursion* ended in an oak.
7. *courier*—An eager *courier* carried the news.
8. *eclipse*—Ray saw notice of an *eclipse* in the news.
9. *installation*—The door comes with free *installation*.
10. *endure*—We can *endure* extra noise and dust for a while.
11. *epistles*—Peter wrote two *epistles*.
12. *nineteenth*—Be sure to read the *nineteenth* verse.
13. *warrior*—An Indian in *warrior* consume rode the pony.
14. *amusing*—They led an *amusing* train.
15. *previous*—It gave a glimpse of *previous* days.
16. *vague*—There was a *vague* bank of fog on the hill.
17. *pneumonia*—Grandfather is prone to *pneumonia.*
18. *abundance*—He had an *abundance* of visitors.
19. *oblige*—He will always *oblige* you with a smile.
20. *chord*—A minor *chord* has a mournful tone.
21. *periodical*—Take a *periodical* survey of the pantry.
22. *hastily*—The *hastily* made cookies were delicious.
23. *acceptable*—Buttermilk is an *acceptable* substitute.
24. *urgent*—Carl's summons was *urgent* but gentle.
25. *contemplate*—Did you *contemplate* the schedule?

LESSON 24
CONTINUED

*See Teacher's Manual for special instructions.

GRADE 5

26. *lonely*—The cat looks *lonely* sitting on the porch.
27. *toward*—Move a little *toward* the door.
28. *quiet*—How *quiet* the house seemed.
29. *ladies*—Three *ladies* picked all the cherries.
30. *drawn*—The children have *drawn* beautiful pictures.
31. *towel*—Hang a clean *towel* on the rod.
32. *coward*—He felt like a *coward* that morning.
33. *powder*—Who spilled *powder* on the floor?
34. *shook*—Mount Sinai *shook* and quaked.
35. *pleasure*—With great *pleasure* I will help you.
36. *tour*—We could *tour* a coal mine.
37. *usual*—March is the *usual* month for wind.
38. *furniture*—That store sells *furniture* and rugs.
39. *rejoice*—Be glad and *rejoice* in the Lord.
40. *Creator*—God is the *Creator* of the earth.
41. *separate*—Keep the spoons *separate* from the forks.
42. *engineer*—The conductor waved to the *engineer*.
43. *salute*—Try to *salute* each day with zest.
44. *religion*—Pure *religion* includes visiting the fatherless.
45. *horror*—I gasped in *horror* at the ugly mess.
46. *altar*—Elijah built an *altar* of stones.
47. *usually*—Some people *usually* eat at five.
48. *generally*—Other people *generally* eat at six.
49. *Jonah*—God told *Jonah* to go to Nineveh.
50. *Micah*—The Book of *Micah* follows Jonah.

GRADE 6

26. *Jerusalem*—The city of David is *Jerusalem*.
27. *preferred*—I would have *preferred* the other one.
28. *influence*—Do not let evil men *influence* you.
29. *produced*—More effort *produced* neater handwriting.
30. *develop*—Be careful not to *develop* bad habits.
31. *garage*—The *garage* door is open.
32. *division*—Do you think long *division* is hard?
33. *bough*—The *bough* of an oak caught Absalom.
34. *measure*—Be sure to *measure* carefully.
35. *nowadays*—Polio is rare *nowadays*.
36. *driven*—The snow was *driven* before the wind.
37. *devout*—Anna was a *devout* woman.
38. *shone*—The sun *shone* brightly through the window.
39. *account*—We must *account* for the lost apples.
40. *sought*—Jesus *sought* to save the lost.
41. *adjustment*—The *adjustment* screw was loose.
42. *baggage*—Take your *baggage* to that counter.
43. *series*—He asked a *series* of questions.
44. *hedge*—That *hedge* needs to be trimmed.
45. *buffalo*—The American *buffalo* is really a bison.
46. *journey*—Jacob made the long *journey* to Egypt.
47. *hygiene*—Good *hygiene* helps us stay well.
48. *scissors*—These *scissors* are sharp.
49. *basis*—On what *basis* did you conclude that?
50. *gentlemen*—Both *gentlemen* left early.

GRADE 4

26. *among*—Divide the crackers *among* the children.
27. *arithmetic*—I checked my *arithmetic* paper.
28. *woman*—A *woman* touched the hem of Jesus' garment.
29. *during*—School is closed *during* the summer.
30. *oranges*—We peeled *oranges* for breakfast.
31. *points*—The compass needle *points* north.
32. *charge*—How much did he *charge* for the bread?
33. *changed*—He must have *changed* his mind.
34. *counter*—The clerk behind the *counter* smiled.
35. *that's*—Yes, *that's* the reason.
36. *holiday*—We have no *holiday* today.
37. *supply*—Forests *supply* the country with wood.
38. *bridge*—Flood waters washed the *bridge* away.
39. *teacher's*—Books are on the *teacher's* desk.
40. *balloon*—My sister's *balloon* burst.
41. *friend's*—We just passed my *friend's* house.
42. *enemy*—The fox is an *enemy* of the rabbit.
43. *enemies*—"Love your *enemies*," Jesus said..
44. *Mennonite*—The sign says *Mennonite* Church.
45. *St.**—Main *Street*
46. *Rd.**—Blue Mountain *Road*
47. *yr.**—twelve months in a *year*
48. *wk.**—seven days in a *week*
49. *mi.**—five thousand, two hundred eighty feet in a *mile*
50. *ft.**—twelve inches in a *foot*

GRADE 7

26. *cooperation*—Firefighters need *cooperation*.
27. *coarse*—We filled *coarse* burlap sacks with corn.
28. *revolution*—Machines brought a new *revolution*.
29. *communication*—Some *communication* is written.
30. *converted*—Paul was *converted* near Damascus.
31. *exceed*—Our income must *exceed* our spending.
32. *remittance*—Send no cash *remittance* in the mail.
33. *conceit*—Haman's *conceit* caused his own downfall.
34. *precede*—Did Lincoln *precede* Johnson as president?
35. *illustrate*—Artists *illustrate* many storybooks.
36. *convenience*—Call at your *convenience*.
37. *relieve*—Allen came to *relieve* the tired watchman.
38. *intercede*—Lawyers *intercede* in behalf of others.
39. *interior*—The earth's *interior* is very hot.
40. *succession*—Four cars in *succession* turned left.
41. *impossible*—The wreck was *impossible* to repair.
42. *aggressive*—Bears are seldom *aggressive* to man.
43. *opponent*—Goliath sneered at his young *opponent*.
44. *constitution*—A *constitution* gives the goals.
45. *negligent*—Eli was a *negligent* father to his sons.
46. *disposition*—His kind *disposition* won friends.
47. *statute*—Every *statute* was voted in by Congress.
48. *gradually*—I *gradually* came to like my new home.
49. *nonresistance*—Dirk showed *nonresistance*.
50. *unnecessary*—Shouting was *unnecessary*.

GRADE 8

26. *dealt*—Winter *dealt* some harsh blows.
27. *paralyze*—Ice will *paralyze* the fan.
28. *precious*—Silence is a *precious* commodity.
29. *conspicuous*—A cricket gave two *conspicuous* chirps.
30. *parachute*—George reached the cliff by *parachute*.
31. *flannel*—He carried *flannel* for the victim.
32. *dehydrate*—How quickly would he *dehydrate*?
33. *geometry*—First grade has *geometry* by learning shapes.
34. *privilege*—It is a *privilege* to live in the country.
35. *occasional*—Take an *occasional* fresh-air walk.
36. *individual*—The children had *individual* garden plots.
37. *magnificent*—Samuel grew a *magnificent* pumpkin.
38. *analysis*—Carver did intense *analysis* of the peanut.
39. *commerce*—Cotton helped to build *commerce* in the South.
40. *hydraulic*—A hose nozzle demonstrates *hydraulic* force.
41. *dreary*—The hall was a *dreary* gray.
42. *unanimous*—There was *unanimous* consent to paint it.
43. *practical*—Choose a *practical* color.
44. *strict*—Mark keeps *strict* watch over the flock.
45. *curiosity*—One lamb's *curiosity* led it astray.
46. *anxiety*—Mark's *anxiety* increased as it grew later.
47. *sufficient*—God's grace is *sufficient* to endure wrong.
48. *vengeance*—We leave *vengeance* in His hands.
49. *theme*—Peace is the *theme* of our relationships.
50. *inferiority*—Submission does not indicate *inferiority*.

LESSON 25

GRADE 2

1. *kind*—"Be ye *kind* one to another."
2. *coat*—Hang up your *coat* and cap.
3. *socks*—Mother is mending *socks* today.
4. *ducks*—See the many *ducks* in the water.
5. *back*—Come *back* again.
6. *seek*—Shepherds *seek* their lost sheep.
7. *block*—A wooden *block* lay on the floor.
8. *cared*—David *cared* for the sheep.
9. *kick*—How far can you *kick* the ball?
10. *lakes*—There are many *lakes* in Minnesota.
11. *cleaning*—Mother is *cleaning* the kitchen.
12. *brick*—A loose *brick* fell from the chimney.

GRADE 5

1. *princess*—The *princess* found baby Moses in the river.
2. *psalm*—David wrote a *psalm* while he tended sheep.
3. *promise*—God keeps every *promise* He makes.
4. *known*—All our needs are *known* to God.
5. *sword*—The Word is the *sword* of the Spirit.
6. *swept*—Sandra *swept* the front porch.
7. *burst*—The lilacs *burst* into bloom.
8. *mistake*—You made a *mistake* in your division.
9. *forced*—The cow was *forced* into the barn.
10. *scarce*—Real silver dollars are *scarce* items.
11. *sense*—The letter did not make any *sense* to her.
12. *acid*—The *acid* ate a hole through the coat.
13. *knew*—I *knew* my answer was not right.
14. *I've*—I don't think *I've* ever seen her.
15. *we've*—Look, *we've* made it to the top.
16. *you've*—Good; *you've* remembered your verse.
    That *certainly* was a *false* report.
    In which *verse* is the *answer* found?

GRADE 6

1. *assemble*—The people will *assemble* here.
2. *prophecy*—Moses spoke a *prophecy* about Christ.
3. *prophesy*—The mob challenged Jesus to *prophesy* to them.
4. *disciples*—The twelve *disciples* followed Jesus.
5. *audience*—Peter preached to a large *audience*.
6. *practice*—Regular *practice* will improve your skill.
7. *grease*—There is *grease* on the floor.
8. *satisfactory*—Your work is *satisfactory* to me.
9. *necessary*—Is this a *necessary* item?
10. *expensive*—The rich man wore *expensive* clothes.
11. *serious*—Saul made a *serious* mistake.
12. *fierce*—Daniel was protected from the *fierce* lions.
13. *happiest*—We are the *happiest* when we obey.
14. *prettiest*—These are the *prettiest* flowers in the garden.
15. *further*—We will discuss the plans *further*.
16. *recently*—They have *recently* moved here.
    His *furious* anger did not *embarrass* her.
    David made *reference* to God's *mercies*.

GRADE 3

1. *pillow*—A soft *pillow* feels good at night.
2. *umbrella*—Take an *umbrella* in case it rains.
3. *kitten*—The lost *kitten* was wet and cold.
4. *seven*—John wrote letters to *seven* churches.
5. *upper*—The disciples were in an *upper* room.
6. *middle*—Psalm 118:8 is the *middle* verse of the Bible.
7. *number*—Their house *number* is 451.
8. *window*—In front of the *window* was a red geranium.
9. *dollar*—The clerk charged one *dollar* for the pen.
10. *forgot*—Someone *forgot* to write his name.
11. *picture*—Draw a *picture* of your house.
12. *lumber*—Men loaded *lumber* onto the railroad car.
13. *twenty*—Grandfather has *twenty* chickens.
14. *getting*—The bees are *getting* nectar from the flowers.
15. *gardens*—People like *gardens* near their houses.
16. *chairs*—There were enough *chairs* for all the people.

GRADE 4

1. *blessing*—We ask a *blessing* on our food.
2. *crossed*—Jesus *crossed* the brook to pray.
3. *mercy*—The lepers said, "Have *mercy* on us."
4. *he'd*—The prodigal son decided *he'd* go back home.
5. *chase*—The dog might *chase* the rabbit.
6. *absent*—Is anyone *absent* today?
7. *I'd*—I believe *I'd* choose green.
8. *space*—The first *space* is called F.
9. *recess*—During *recess* we play tag.
10. *answer*—Jesus gave the men a good *answer*.
11. *grown*—Many potatoes are *grown* in Idaho.
12. *lace*—Flowers are prettier than *lace* and ribbons.
13. *blew*—An east wind *blew* locusts into Egypt.
14. *since*—Arizona is desert, *since* it is hot and dry.
15. *cents*—One hundred *cents* make a dollar.
16. *nurse*—The doctor told the *nurse* what to write.

The bell *rang twice*.

Blue flowers *grew* in the hanging *basket*.

GRADE 7

1. *corpse*—Jesus raised a *corpse* to life.
2. *manual*—Read the *manual* for directions.
3. *carnality*—Envy is a form of *carnality*.
4. *baptized*—Jesus was *baptized* in the Jordan River.
5. *corrupt*—Sodom was a very *corrupt* city.
6. *associate*—We usually *associate* salt with pepper.
7. *criticize*—The Pharisees did *criticize* Jesus.
8. *manufacturer*—This *manufacturer* makes paper products.
9. *capitalization*—Titles need *capitalization*.
10. *certificate*—His *certificate* hung on the wall.
11. *encourage*—We *encourage* proper reading habits.
12. *merchandise*—A store displays its *merchandise*.
13. *commemorate*—We *commemorate* the resurrection.
14. *identify*—Can you *identify* twenty different birds?
15. *Christendom*—All *Christendom* claims to believe the Bible.
16. *cordial*—The Yoders gave us all a *cordial* welcome.
17. *Incarnation*—Christ became a man through the *Incarnation*.
18. *consequently*—Lassie barked; *consequently*, John awoke.
19. *corporal*—Mr. Taylor was an army *corporal*.
20. *justify*—Good works alone do not *justify* us.
21. *endeavor*—We must *endeavor* to do our best.
22. *corporation*—A new *corporation* moved into town.
23. *manager*—Daniel is a sales *manager* for the company.
24. *extension*—We lengthened it with an *extension*.
25. *corps*—A group of trained soldiers is a *corps*.

GRADE 8

1. *immigrant*—Each *immigrant* had a health examination.
2. *susceptible*—Children are *susceptible* to mischief.
3. *unregenerate*—Christ came to save *unregenerate* man.
4. *nitrogen*—Read the *nitrogen* content of the fertilizer.
5. *defendant*—Jesus had no *defendant* before Pilate.
6. *inhabitant*—One thief is now an *inhabitant* of heaven.
7. *testimony*—His *testimony* of guilt was sincere.
8. *triumph*—He shares in the *triumph* of the resurrection.
9. *architect*—Who was the *architect* of this staircase?
10. *superintendent*—Contact the building *superintendent*.
11. *tourist*—It is a popular *tourist* attraction.
12. *scientist*—Faith is mystery to a *scientist*.
13. *generate*—Faith can *generate* miracles.
14. *enthusiastic*—There was *enthusiastic* scrubbing in the hall.
15. *solvent*—A bit of *solvent* erased black marks.
16. *responsibility*—We'll take *responsibility* to keep it clean.
17. *typist*—Hudson Bank needs a new *typist*.
18. *applicant*—Has there been any *applicant* for the job?
19. *attendant*—The governor's *attendant* called a taxi.
20. *consultant*—A special *consultant* shared the ride.
21. *therapist*—His *therapist* called for more exercise.
22. *oxygen*—Get more *oxygen* in your lungs.
23. *ornament*—Wear the *ornament* of meekness.
24. *hydrogen*—The largest element of water is *hydrogen*.
25. *violent*—The shed collapsed in *violent* winds.

LESSON 26

1. *stick*—We glue pictures to make them *stick* to the paper.
2. *soft*—"A *soft* answer turneth away wrath."
3. *city*—The lights in the *city* seem very bright.
4. *sorry*—We are *sorry* that you are sick.
5. *nice*—Grandmother's flowers look *nice*, don't they?
6. *ice*—How thick is the *ice* on the river?
7. *place*—I know whose *place* this is.
8. *pass*—Please *pass* the butter.
9. *last*—The *last* one in should close the door.
10. *talks*—Mother *talks* kindly to us.
11. *swing*—You may play on the *swing* first.
12. *once*—Only *once* did we hear the noise.

GRADE 5

1. *you'd*—Here is a book *you'd* like.
2. *who's*—I wonder *who's* here.
3. *permitted*—Anthony was *permitted* to help.
4. *baptize*—The bishops *baptize* the believers.
5. *measles*—Did you have *measles* yet?
6. *resort*—Parents are your *resort* in trouble.
7. *blaze*—The *blaze* from the fireplace was inviting.
8. *lazy*—A *lazy* person loses many blessings.
9. *puzzle*—The *puzzle* looked nice when it was together.
10. *chose*—God *chose* Moses to lead His people.
11. *chosen*—Ministers are *chosen* men of God.
12. *arise*—Never let ill feelings *arise* within you.
13. *arose*—Jesus *arose* from the dead.
14. *freeze*—Do you *freeze* all your meat?
15. *froze*—The plants *froze* last night.
16. *frozen*—The pond was *frozen* over.

    Whose home is in the middle of the *desert*?
    A *dozen* letters would surely *surprise* him.

GRADE 6

1. *business*—This is a *business* street.
2. *baptism*—Jesus' *baptism* was an example for us.
3. *baptized*—He was *baptized* in the Jordan River.
4. *composition*—This *composition* is well written.
5. *unpleasant*—We had an *unpleasant* experience.
6. *exactly*—Do *exactly* as I showed you.
7. *example*—Be an *example* to others.
8. *dessert*—Do you want your *dessert* later?
9. *blizzard*—A *blizzard* was raging outside.
10. *citizen*—Paul was a Roman *citizen*.
11. *disease*—Naaman had the *disease* of leprosy.
12. *vice-president*—Our *vice-president* is in Washington.
13. *advertised*—The book was *advertised* here.
14. *opposite*—You do the *opposite* of what I do.
15. *there's*—She said *there's* a box in here.
16. *theirs*—The money was *theirs* to keep.

    They're using *poison* to kill the weeds.
    The *puzzle represented* nothing at all.

GRADE 3

1. *can't*—An engine *can't* run without fuel.
2. *he'll*—The man said *he'll* come again.
3. *I'm*—I know *I'm* older than you.
4. *he's*—Our neighbor said *he's* sick again.
5. *she'll*—Ruth said *she'll* help.
6. *don't*—Why *don't* you look under the table?
7. *isn't*—The clock *isn't* working any more.
8. *we'll*—I suppose *we'll* mow the lawn.
9. *she's*—Ask Rachel what *she's* planning.
10. *you'll*—Soon *you'll* see the ocean.
11. *Mr.*—A farmer rents *Mr.* Jergen's land.
12. *Mrs.*—Mother gave a pie to *Mrs.* Berk.
13. *Miss*—The lady said she is *Miss* Cooley.
14. *dollar*—Will one *dollar* buy a new book?
15. *picture*—A pretty *picture* hangs on the wall.
16. *twenty*—Donald has *twenty* post cards.

GRADE 4

1. *praise*—Psalm 8 is a psalm of *praise* to God.
2. *children*—"Hosanna!" the *children* sang.
3. *led*—Moses *led* the Israelites out of Egypt.
4. *presents*—Wise men brought *presents* to Jesus.
5. *women*—The Bible says that *women* should not preach.
6. *wisdom*—How much better is *wisdom* than gold!
7. *noise*—"Make a joyful *noise* unto the LORD."
8. *easy*—Was that word *easy* to spell?
9. *taught*—Jesus *taught* as one having authority.
10. *slept*—The bear *slept* all winter.
11. *hose*—With a kink in the *hose*, water cannot flow.
12. *mouse*—Joy put butter on the trap to catch the *mouse*.
13. *teeth*—Your four front *teeth* are called incisors.
14. *dozen*—One and one-half *dozen* is eighteen.
15. *reasons*—There are two *reasons* he cannot come.
16. *desert*—Northern Africa is mostly *desert* land.

 A boy *bought* two *mice* for his kittens.
 This red line shows the *size* of the *zone*.

GRADE 7

1. *hearty*—Brother Ben gave me a *hearty* handshake.
2. *fraternity*—The *fraternity* had twelve members.
3. *affiliate*—Do *affiliate* with wholesome friends.
4. *emphasize*—We need to *emphasize* brotherly love.
5. *patriot*—Patrick Henry was an early American *patriot*.
6. *humility*—Pride is the opposite of *humility*.
7. *remedy*—Naaman found no *remedy* for leprosy in Syria.
8. *bargain*—We struck a *bargain* with the trader.
9. *majority*—The *majority* of animals are insects.
10. *iniquity*—Dishonesty is an *iniquity* before God.
11. *matrimony*—Holy *matrimony* was ordained by God.
12. *patron*—The grocery store gave each *patron* a pen.
13. *maternal*—Aunt Hilda is a loving, *maternal* woman.
14. *dignity*—Begging was beneath the debtor's *dignity*.
15. *difficulty*—Emily is having *difficulty* with reading.
16. *difference*—What is the *difference* between the two?
17. *fiery*—Who was cast into the *fiery* furnace?
18. *physical*—Something *physical* can be seen or felt.
19. *misery*—Sin has brought great *misery* to man.
20. *prophesy*—Who will *prophesy* for the Lord?
21. *paternal*—Only my *paternal* grandfather is still living.
22. *filial*—We have *filial* ties to our parents.
23. *tariff*—Tax on foreign goods is a *tariff*.
24. *patriarch*—Abraham was a *patriarch* of old.
25. *fraternal*—Jan and Ann are *fraternal* twins.

GRADE 8

1. *career*—Describe your *career* in the kitchen.
2. *brochure*—Read this *brochure* on canning.
3. *restaurant*—Some tips were used in the *restaurant*.
4. *available*—They are *available* to all the workers.
5. *juvenile*—Debbie is a *juvenile* cook.
6. *corsage*—Kim gave Mother a *corsage* of violets.
7. *croquet*—She found them during the *croquet* game.
8. *amateur*—Frank is an *amateur* carpenter.
9. *fatigue*—Heavy work causes *fatigue*.
10. *employee*—Each *employee* can help encourage the others.
11. *referee*—Do the ants have a *referee*?
12. *beige*—Please clean the *beige* carpet again.
13. *bouquet*—The daffodil *bouquet* drank all its water.
14. *sunset*—We sang until *sunset*.
15. *engineer*—The *engineer* let us blow the whistle.
16. *chaperon*—Uncle Ben was our *chaperon* at the zoo.
17. *lieutenant*—He met a *lieutenant* from his service days.
18. *parliament*—The last session of *parliament* was short.
19. *revenue*—They will need more *revenue* next year.
20. *chauffeur*—The new *chauffeur* missed his road.
21. *compliment*—Jean gave him a *compliment* for safe driving.
22. *silhouette*—The tree was a *silhouette* in the moonlight.
23. *camouflage*—Shadows helped to *camouflage* the antelope.
24. *gourmet*—Bees in the desert make *gourmet* honey.
25. *souvenir*—We took a tiny cactus as a *souvenir*.

LESSON 27

GRADE 2

1. *walking*—Jesus was *walking* along the road.
2. *while*—The disciples listened *while* Jesus spoke.
3. *where*—People went to the place *where* Jesus was.
4. *when*—We do not know *when* Jesus will come again.
5. *warm*—The sunshine feels *warm* on my back.
6. *wake*—Did you *wake* during the night?
7. *woods*—The trees in the *woods* are wet from the rain.
8. *why*—We know *why* the floor is dirty.
9. *win*—We like to play games whether we *win* or lose.
10. *wind*—See the *wind* blowing the trees.
11. *wild*—A tiger is a *wild* animal.
12. *what*—Listen to *what* he says.

*See Teacher's Manual for special instructions.

GRADE 5

1. *they're*—If *they're* home, we will visit them.
2. *zero*—It was thirty below *zero* in the North.
3. *collect*—I will *collect* the papers to check them.
4. *electric*—The fan runs by an *electric* motor.
5. *secretary*—The *secretary* read the latest report.
6. *wreck*—There was a *wreck* at the crossroad.
7. *stroke*—One more *stroke* and the tree will fall.
8. *echo*—He heard his *echo* bounce back to him.
9. *conduct*—Always *conduct* yourself wisely.
10. *potatoes*—We plant *potatoes* every year.
11. *struck*—The lightning *struck* the tree.
12. *keeper*—A wife should be a *keeper* at home.
13. *folks*—The older *folks* enjoyed the singing.
14. *speaker*—The *speaker* had a clear voice.
15. *tomatoes*—The *tomatoes* were big and red.
16. *escape*—God helped David to *escape* from Saul.

  Their tractor needs to be fixed.
  You're not to lie on your *stomach* yet.

GRADE 6

1. *brook*—That *brook* is deep.
2. *clerk*—The *clerk* sold a broom.
3. *pickles*—Do you want *pickles* on your sandwich?
4. *choir*—The *choir* sang to the old people.
5. *acquaint*—Please *acquaint* me with your plans.
6. *equipment*—Did you bring your *equipment* along?
7. *qualified*—He is a *qualified* surgeon.
8. *qualities*—Honesty and courtesy are two important *qualities*.
9. *occur*—Did this ever *occur* before?
10. *connected*—The wire is not *connected* to the box.
11. *instruction*—The Bible contains much *instruction* for us.
12. *court*—The *court* will decide who is guilty.
13. *kerosene*—The jug is full of *kerosene*.
14. *respectable*—She led a very *respectable* life.
15. *overlook*—God will not *overlook* sin.
16. *yourselves*—You *yourselves* know what happened.

  According to him, they had a *quarrel*.*
  The man is *securing* the *electrical* wire.

GRADE 3

1. *Ruth*—The Book of *Ruth* has four chapters.
2. *1 Kings*—In *1 Kings* we read about Solomon.
3. *2 Kings*—In *2 Kings* we read about Elisha.
4. *Job*—The Book of *Job* comes before Psalms.
5. *Mark*—Yes, *Mark* is in the New Testament.
6. *Luke*—The Golden Rule is in *Luke* 6:31.
7. *John*—We all know *John* 3:16.
8. *Acts*—The Book of *Acts* follows John.
9. *James*—The Book of *James* follows Hebrews.
10. *1 Peter*—The Book of *1 Peter* has five chapters.
11. *2 Peter*—The Book of *2 Peter* has three chapters.
12. *Jude*—The Book of *Jude* is second to last.
13. *holy*—God used *holy* men to write the Scriptures.
14. *isn't*—The cup *isn't* full of water.
15. *don't*—Tomatoes *don't* grow well in the shade.
16. *we'll*—Sometime *we'll* see Jesus.

GRADE 4

1. *we're*—Now *we're* ready to begin.
2. *pictures*—The Bible gives many *pictures* of heaven.
3. *carrying*—The dog is *carrying* your shoe away.
4. *pocketbook*—The lady's *pocketbook* is lost.
5. *it's*—Yes, *it's* your turn.
6. *chickens*—Male *chickens* are called roosters.
7. *trunk*—Sap flows through the *trunk* of a tree.
8. *stockings*—Two *stockings* make a pair.
9. *music*—The chirping of birds is *music* to my ear.
10. *skates*—A Dutch boy *skates* on the frozen canal.
11. *Christmas*—In Peru, *Christmas* is in summer.
12. *forgave*—Jesus *forgave* the people who hurt Him.
13. *break*—In heaven, thieves do not *break* through.
14. *forgotten*—Joseph had not *forgotten* Jacob.
15. *choose*—David went to *choose* five stones.
16. *broke*—Gideon's men *broke* their pitchers.

The walls *crack* when the houses *shake*.
After we clean the *kitchen*, we will go on a *picnic*.*

GRADE 7

1. *equine*—Bridles and reins are *equine* gear.
2. *involved*—Our assignment *involved* much reading.
3. *feline*—Tigers are members of the *feline* family.
4. *bass*—Jonathan has a deep *bass* voice.
5. *rite*—Feet Washing is a *rite* commanded by Christ.
6. *canary*—The yellow *canary* sang sweetly.
7. *indebtedness*—We feel *indebtedness* to God.
8. *textile*—Cloth comes from the *textile* mills.
9. *feminine*—Roberta is the *feminine* form of Robert.
10. *canine*—Dogs and wolves belong to the *canine* family.
11. *covenant*—Israel broke her *covenant* to serve God.
12. *infantile*—The baby made gurgling, *infantile* sounds.
13. *census*—A man came to collect *census* information.
14. *vaccine*—Polio *vaccine* has reduced that disease.
15. *masculine*—"He" and "his" are *masculine* pronouns.
16. *cereal*—We ate oatmeal *cereal* for breakfast.
17. *versatile*—Wood is a useful, *versatile* material.
18. *minor*—Do not let *minor* disagreements disturb you.
19. *council*—The village *council* met every month.
20. *vein*—A blood *vein* carries blood to the heart.
21. *reptile*—An alligator is a *reptile*.
22. *counsel*—Rehoboam asked the young men for *counsel*.
23. *domestic*—Dusting furniture is a *domestic* chore.
24. *circumstances*—Absalom lived in pleasant *circumstances*.
25. *doubtless*—I knew that, *doubtless*, I would be late.

GRADE 8

1. *flourish*—Joel swings his bat with a *flourish*.
2. *boulevard*—The *boulevard* was littered with leaves.
3. *accompany*—Did the kitten *accompany* the rabbit?
4. *alarm*—The fire *alarm* rang.
5. *galloped*—Frantic children *galloped* down the hall.
6. *maneuver*—We need to practice that *maneuver* again.
7. *camouflage*—Flowers can *camouflage* a weathered fence.
8. *warrant*—Bad paint does not *warrant* a new fence.
9. *guaranteed*—Use paint that is *guaranteed* to cover rust.
10. *sabotage*—The property showed signs of *sabotage*.
11. *picturesque*—Roses make a *picturesque* arbor.
12. *prairie*—Summer was dry on the *prairie*.
13. *reservoir*—The pond made a *reservoir* for irrigating.
14. *anoint*—God asked Samuel to *anoint* a new king.
15. *deem*—He did not *deem* Saul worthy to continue.
16. *exhibition*—Patrick held an *exhibition* of metals.
17. *galvanized*—Chemical reaction *galvanized* the nails.
18. *garage*—He sold them at the *garage* sale.
19. *bureau*—I found a used *bureau* in the corner.
20. *campaign*—Moses did not *campaign* for his charge.
21. *fraud*—Pharaoh's magicians were a *fraud*.
22. *adjourned*—The king's court *adjourned* in embarrassment.
23. *madam*—Let the *madam* go first.
24. *mutton*—She ordered *mutton* from the butcher.
25. *asterisk*—An *asterisk* marks this week's special.

LESSON 28

GRADE 2

1. *larger*—Lima beans are *larger* than peas.
2. *bigger*—Some cabbage heads are *bigger* than others.
3. *better*—Tomatoes like sunshine *better* than shade.
4. *best*—Bananas grow *best* in warm climates.
5. *more*—Mother bought *more* eggs at the store.
6. *dark*—Stars look bright on a *dark* night.
7. *most*—The smallest rosebush had the *most* flowers.
8. *much*—"Thank you very *much*," he said.
9. *harder*—Try *harder* before you give up.
10. *warmer*—Afternoons are usually *warmer* than forenoons.
11. *higher*—Raise your hand *higher* so that I can see it.
12. *highest*—The squirrel climbed to the *highest* branch.

GRADE 5

1. *shouldn't*—You *shouldn't* laugh at others' mistakes.
2. *quite*—The rock was *quite* difficult to move.
3. *oxen*—Two *oxen* pulled the wooden cart.
4. *chairman*—The *chairman* was late for the meeting.
5. *expect*—Do you *expect* rain soon?
6. *extend*—Father wants to *extend* the fence.
7. *quietly*—Mother *quietly* rocked the baby.
8. *reward*—Balaam wanted a *reward*.
9. *quilt*—We are making a *quilt* for her.
10. *policeman*—One *policeman* waved us on past.
11. *excitement*—The fire caused much *excitement* that night.
12. *exercise*—Plenty of *exercise* is good for your health.
13. *unexpected*—The *unexpected* noise scared her.
14. *headquarters*—Go to the *headquarters* for orders.
15. *except*—We work every day *except* Sunday.
16. *backward*—Lot's wife gave a *backward* look.

Wouldn't he be able to run, or *doesn't* he want to?
The poor pony *couldn't* understand my *language*.

GRADE 6

1. *width*—We measured the *width* of the room.
2. *weapon*—David's *weapon* was a sling.
3. *watchful*—"Be *watchful*," the Bible tells us.
4. *forwarding*—I am *forwarding* this letter to you.
5. *exclaimed*—"What?" *exclaimed* Father.
6. *expedition*—The *expedition* was successful.
7. *experience*—I do not have *experience* in that work.
8. *excess*—There was an *excess* of noise.
9. *accept*—Will you *accept* this gift?
10. *accident*—They had an *accident* today.
11. *express*—Let me *express* my thanks.
12. *meanwhile*—There was a delay, so, *meanwhile*, I read.
13. *whatever*—You should do *whatever* he does.
14. *elsewhere*—Please move this box *elsewhere*.
15. *whirl*—Watch the top *whirl* around.
16. *worthy*—I am not *worthy* of your kindness.

Do you know *whether* we should do this *exercise*?
In his *excitement* he failed to *weigh* the matter.

GRADE 3

1. *your*—Use *your* own pencil.
2. *yourself*—Try it *yourself* before you ask for help.
3. *every*—That dog barks at *every* car.
4. *everyday*—Change into your *everyday* clothes.
5. *whenever*—Come *whenever* you can.
6. *airplane*—We heard an *airplane* overhead.
7. *birthday*—On Ben's next *birthday* he will be ten.
8. *windmill*—The *windmill* turned swiftly in the wind.
9. *rainbow*—We saw a *rainbow* in the sky.
10. *snowman*—The *snowman* was taller than the children.
11. *daylight*—We arose before *daylight* that morning.
12. *doorway*—Ann stopped at the *doorway* to say good-bye.
13. *sidewalk*—Ice on a *sidewalk* is dangerous.
14. *2 Kings*—The Book of *2 Kings* tells about Naaman.
15. *Job*—The Book of *Job* follows Esther.
16. *Acts*—In *Acts* we read about Stephen.

GRADE 4

1. *checks*—See the pretty *checks* in the tablecloth.
2. *cracks*—A cold jar *cracks* in hot water.
3. *square*—A *square* has four equal sides.
4. *unlike*—It is *unlike* Alvin to be late.
5. *wax*—When should we *wax* the floor?
6. *disorderly*—Clean up your *disorderly* desk.
7. *language*—In the French *language,* "et" means "and."
8. *Thanksgiving*——*Thanksgiving* Day is in the fall.
9. *discolored*—Sunlight *discolored* the paper.
10. *unpainted*—They bought *unpainted* furniture.
11. *mixed*—Red and yellow *mixed* make orange.
12. *weather*—God controls the *weather* every day.
13. *sixteen*—Who knows the first *sixteen* verses?
14. *question*—God asked Job a *question* about snow.
15. *quickly*—"Arise up *quickly,*" the angel told Peter.
16. *broken*—The fish had not *broken* the net.

We *wondered* what animals made such large *tracks.*
Father *kept* his head covered as he *watched* the bees.

GRADE 7

1. *chorus*—Outside, a *chorus* of birds was singing.
2. *junior*—Mr. Clark was only a *junior* officer.
3. *particularly*—Jason was not *particularly* fond of olives.
4. *attached*—A note was *attached* to the box.
5. *juvenile*—The book is too *juvenile* for teenagers.
6. *adventure*—Sleeping outside was a real *adventure.*
7. *kitchenette*—We ate in the tiny *kitchenette.*
8. *senile*—The elderly man seemed to be *senile* and ill.
9. *boundary*—The ball bounced over the *boundary* line.
10. *ringlet*—Jane touched a *ringlet* of the baby's hair.
11. *pamphlet*—I received a small *pamphlet* in the mail.
12. *cassette*—Barbara listened to a *cassette* tape.
13. *redemption*—Coupon *redemption* can save money.
14. *molecule*—A water *molecule* has hydrogen and oxygen.
15. *schedule*—Math class comes first on our *schedule.*
16. *characters*—Moses and Elijah are famous Bible *characters.*
17. *senator*—A state *senator* helps make new laws.
18. *phrase*—I remember only one *phrase* of the new song.
19. *chemistry*—In *chemistry* I learned about elements.
20. *senior*—Charles is a *senior* partner in that company.
21. *rejuvenate*—Rest can *rejuvenate* a tired body.
22. *dinette*—Their *dinette* set had a table and six chairs.
23. *booklet*—Our list of addresses is in a *booklet.*
24. *paragraph*—Read the first *paragraph* aloud.
25. *joyful*—An angel brought *joyful* news to Mary.

GRADE 8

1. *ambitious*—One *ambitious* gopher ventured too far.
2. *coyote*—He provided dinner for a *coyote.*
3. *cafeteria*—The meadow *cafeteria* was wide and sunny.
4. *pirate*—A swarthy *pirate* boarded the victim ship.
5. *recommended*—The captain *recommended* that he repent.
6. *resources*—Seek more honorable *resources* than theft.
7. *desirous*—Aren't we all *desirous* of a good conscience?
8. *maiden*—We saw a frail *maiden* in a grove.
9. *hammock*—She was swinging her sister in a *hammock.*
10. *continuously*—They were *continuously* smiling.
11. *alligator*—Fashion has endangered the *alligator.*
12. *valuable*—Its hide made *valuable* leather.
13. *miscellaneous*—It was used in *miscellaneous* articles.
14. *tendency*—Resist the *tendency* to criticize.
15. *conscientious*—A *conscientious* effort deserves reward.
16. *plaza*—The shop across the *plaza* opened early.
17. *continuous*—There was a *continuous* flow of customers.
18. *strenuous*—The merchant had a *strenuous* day.
19. *pamphlets*—His free *pamphlets* were gone by noon.
20. *barbecue*—Jason fixed *barbecue* for dinner.
21. *preparation*—The *preparation* took longer than usual.
22. *voluntary*—Susan gave some *voluntary* help.
23. *associated*—This menu is often *associated* with picnics.
24. *barbarous*—A picnic is no excuse for *barbarous* manners.
25. *occasionally*—Check your records *occasionally.*

LESSON 29

GRADE 2

1. *dinner*—Before we eat *dinner*, we wash our hands.
2. *apples*—Red and yellow *apples* are in the bowl.
3. *hidden*—The mother cat has *hidden* her kittens.
4. *spell*—We know how to *spell* many words.
5. *still*—Sit *still* and listen.
6. *fell*—Big raindrops *fell* from the sky.
7. *add*—We can *add* and subtract.
8. *kettle*—Mother filled the *kettle* with soup.
9. *off*—Take the lid *off* the jar.
10. *called*—Robert *called* to his dog.
11. *across*—Can you jump *across* the stream?
12. *happy*—The children are *happy* to play together.

*See Teacher's Manual for special instructions.

GRADE 5

1. *hadn't*—I *hadn't* done my work.
2. *hasn't*—He *hasn't* planted beans yet.
3. *yield*—Our trees *yield* apples and pears.
4. *million*—A *million* people is a great multitude.
5. *knives*—The mower *knives* need sharpening.
6. *velvet*—Feel the soft, *velvet* pillow.
7. *removed*—We have *removed* all the old paint.
8. *grave*—A *grave* used to be dug by hand.
9. *unite*—We like to *unite* our voices in singing.
10. *ourselves*—Do we see *ourselves* as we are?
11. *leavened*—The *leavened* bread was made with yeast.
12. *whether*—He doesn't know *whether* he will go.
13. *thieves*—Two *thieves* were crucified with Jesus.
14. *vow*—Jephthah made a rash *vow* to God.
15. *whisper*—We can *whisper* a prayer to God.
16. *union*—The marriage *union* was planned by God.

Place this *whistle* on that pile of six red *handkerchiefs*.

The men saw the *Saviour themselves* long ago.

GRADE 6

1. *volume*—Find the *volume* of this box.
2. *accurate*—Be sure to do *accurate* work.
3. *kneel*—The Hebrews would not *kneel* to the image.
4. *knowledge*—Solomon had *knowledge* about many things.
5. *onion*—Put an *onion* in the stew.
6. *companion*—His only *companion* was a book.
7. *universal*—Father replaced the *universal* joint.
8. *beyond*—We must live *beyond* what we see.
9. *honesty*—Your *honesty* is refreshing.
10. *humble*—Moses was a *humble* man.
11. *honestly*—The statement was *honestly* made.
12. *peck**—We bought a *peck* of apples.
13. *bushel**—We needed a *bushel* of potatoes too.
14. *millimeter**—A *millimeter* is a small measurement.
15. *milligram**—Every day, we need one *milligram* of vitamin B₁.
16. *Boulevard**—Jeffrey lives along Dogwood *Boulevard*.

The *lawyer* must know who the *heir* will be.

Failure is *regularly* caused by poor planning.

GRADE 3

1. *early*—Abraham rose up *early* in the morning.
2. *earth*—The *earth* is the Lord's.
3. *world*—God created the *world* in six days.
4. *hurry*—The mailman tried to *hurry* on his way.
5. *learning*—We are *learning* interesting things.
6. *burned*—Harold *burned* the trash yesterday.
7. *fur*—Rabbit *fur* is soft.
8. *dirty*—No one likes *dirty* floors.
9. *thirty*—Mother canned *thirty* quarts of pears.
10. *fir*—A row of *fir* trees marked the boundary.
11. *hurt*—Was anyone *hurt* badly?
12. *shirt*—Hang the *shirt* on a hanger.
13. *dirt*—Sweep the *dirt* into a pile.
14. *airplane*—Have you had an *airplane* ride?
15. *rainbow*—Draw a *rainbow* with seven colors.
16. *doorway*—Do not stand in the *doorway* to talk.

GRADE 4

1. *wooden*—Rails are fastened to *wooden* ties.
2. *gloves*—This pair of *gloves* is made of wool.
3. *yoke*—The two oxen have a *yoke* around their necks.
4. *which*—Choose *which* Bible story we shall read.
5. *discover*—A plumber could *discover* the trouble.
6. *awhile*—Sit down *awhile* until we are ready.
7. *fearful*—The broken glass was a *fearful* sight.
8. *remove*—Come in and *remove* your wraps.
9. *whistle*—A train *whistle* sounded nearby.
10. *vacation*—During *vacation*, remember to read.
11. *careful*—"Oh, be *careful*, little hands, what you do."
12. *silver*—God knew about the *silver* Achan stole.
13. *twelve*—Jacob had *twelve* sons.
14. *youngest*—David was Jesse's *youngest* son.
15. *golden*—The king held out his *golden* scepter.
16. *salvation*—Jesus brought *salvation* to mankind.

Do your work *yourself whenever* you can.
Our minister was *thankful* that we *visited* him.

GRADE 7

1. *mosquitoes*—Many *mosquitoes* buzzed around.
2. *ancient*—Pyramids are *ancient* Egyptian tombs.
3. *physician*—Luke was a *physician* in Bible times.
4. *feasible*—A round earth was *feasible* to Columbus.
5. *courteous*—Nabal was neither *courteous* nor kind.
6. *proportion*—Draw objects in proper *proportion*.
7. *agriculture*—David liked *agriculture*.
8. *descent*—The *descent* was breathtaking.
9. *assistant*—The dental *assistant* x-rayed Dale's teeth.
10. *sheriff*—A county *sheriff* enforces law and order.
11. *analyze*—Scientists *analyze* the needs of the soil.
12. *judgment*—Jethro's good *judgment* helped Moses.
13. *committee*—The *committee* planned the menu.
14. *argument*—The boys had an *argument*.
15. *muscle*—God made *muscle* cells long and thin.
16. *temperature*—Joel's *temperature* was rising.
17. *atmosphere*—Gases make up our *atmosphere*.
18. *mystery*—Gravity is still a *mystery* to man.
19. *wherever*—Paul went *wherever* God led him.
20. *category*—Each *category* of insects in interesting.
21. *occurrence*—Rain is a daily *occurrence* there.
22. *impulsive*—Peter made an *impulsive* promise.
23. *congratulate*—We want to *congratulate* him.
24. *ordinary*—Seventy years is an *ordinary* life span.
25. *cooperation*—Good *cooperation* is needed.

GRADE 8

1. *iguana*—You will not find the *iguana* in the Arctic.
2. *hurricane*—Neither is a *hurricane* from the north.
3. *Anabaptist*—Jan is well read in *Anabaptist* history.
4. *omitted*—The state church *omitted* some basic truths.
5. *propaganda*—*Propaganda* was used against believers.
6. *visitors*—The factory will give *visitors* a tour any time.
7. *unnecessary*—Previous notice is *unnecessary*.
8. *partial*—Some days they have only *partial* operation.
9. *capitalism*—Factories thrive under *capitalism*.
10. *patio*—We relaxed on the *patio* after dark.
11. *mosquito*—Itchy *mosquito* bites spoiled the pleasure.
12. *avocado*—Have you tried *avocado* salad?
13. *preference*—Bill's *preference* is tomato salad.
14. *outstanding*—Combine them for an *outstanding* treat.
15. *submarine*—Mark painted a *submarine* view.
16. *attached*—Many barnacles were *attached* to the rocks.
17. *stampede*—Indians used the *stampede* as a hunting aid.
18. *canyon*—They ran buffalo over a *canyon* rim.
19. *communism*—The tribal system was a form of *communism*.
20. *suicide*—Could the wreck have been a *suicide*?
21. *criticism*—Surrounding evidence puts *criticism* on that idea.
22. *tornado*—God gave the *tornado* unique power.
23. *rheumatism*—A dry climate eases *rheumatism*.
24. *meter*—The wise person will *meter* his spending.
25. *maintenance*—A working budget takes *maintenance*.

LESSON 30

GRADE 2

1. *back*—Come *back* to where you started.
2. *coat*—My *coat* has big pockets.
3. *kick*—That cow might *kick*; so stay back.
4. *seek*—We will *seek* until we find it.
5. *cleaning*—The girls are *cleaning* the house today.
6. *soft*—How *soft* the rabbit feels!
7. *place*—The Keeners' *place* is along this road.
8. *swing*—The wind made the sign *swing* back and forth.
9. *pass*—Quietly *pass* to your seats.
10. *city*—Houses in a *city* are close together.
11. *wild*—A lion is a *wild* animal.
12. *what*—Do you know *what* I did?
13. *when*—We get up *when* Mother calls.
14. *warm*—Coats keep us *warm* when it is cold.
15. *where*—This is *where* we learn our lesson.
16. *harder*—Some lessons are *harder* than others.
17. *better*—Ripe peaches taste *better* than green ones.
18. *much*—Ask how *much* it costs.
19. *highest*—What was the *highest* temperature yesterday?
20. *bigger*—We need a *bigger* box.
21. *across*—The ferry goes *across* the lake.
22. *dinner*—Some visitors ate *dinner* with us.
23. *spell*—Be sure to *spell* your name right.
24. *apples*—The jars are full of *apples* and cherries.
25. *add*—We *add* to find the sum.

GRADE 5

1. *grave*—Jesus was in the *grave* three days.
2. *removed*—The angels *removed* the stone.
3. *knew*—Then the women *knew* that Jesus had risen.
4. *mistake*—God never makes a *mistake*.
5. *froze*—The water *froze* in the pipes.
6. *quite*—It is *quite* possible that a storm will come.
7. *lazy*—Smoke rose from chimneys in *lazy* circles.
8. *folks*—How many *folks* live there?
9. *arise*—The angel told Elijah to *arise* and eat.
10. *expect*—We *expect* the Lord to return soon.
11. *frozen*—Several cakes are *frozen* in the freezer.
12. *chose*—The girls *chose* apple pie.
13. *ourselves*—We must do the work *ourselves*.
14. *conduct*—Try to *conduct* yourself mannerly.
15. *collect*—You may *collect* all the scissors.
16. *vow*—A person who is baptized makes a *vow* to God.
17. *knives*—Sharpen the *knives* so that they cut better.
18. *unite*—"Come, let us all *unite* to sing."
19. *psalm*—Read a *psalm* for devotions.
20. *baptize*—The bishop will *baptize* the boys.
21. *echo*—Hear the *echo* bounce back from the barn.
22. *princess*—A king's daughter is a *princess*.
23. *million*—The sky was lit with a *million* stars.
24. *forced*—A machine *forced* air into the tube.
25. *policeman*—Wait until the *policeman* motions to us.

GRADE 6

1. *grease*—The pioneers often used bear *grease*.
2. *further*—We plan to investigate *further* tomorrow.
3. *prophecy*—Elisha's *prophecy* was fulfilled.
4. *expensive*—That is too *expensive* for us.
5. *disciples*—Then the *disciples* were glad indeed.
6. *satisfactory*—Those plans are *satisfactory*.
7. *audience*—Look at the *audience* as you speak.
8. *fierce*—The devil is a *fierce* adversary.
9. *necessary*—How much sugar is *necessary*?
10. *prettiest*—Which do you think are the *prettiest* flowers?
11. *baptism*—Glen was ready for *baptism*.
12. *business*—This is called a *business* letter.
13. *example*—Be a good *example* to others.
14. *composition*—This *composition* is too short.
15. *blizzard*—The *blizzard* came up very quickly.
16. *unpleasant*—Present chastening is *unpleasant*.
17. *dessert*—That *dessert* was delicious.
18. *vice-president*—The *vice-president* of the board was absent.
19. *disease*—Naaman had the *disease* of leprosy.
20. *acquaint*—*Acquaint* yourself with truth.
21. *theirs*—This table is *theirs* for today.
22. *instruction*—Follow each *instruction* carefully.
23. *clerk*—The *clerk* wrapped my package.
24. *equipment*—Keep your *equipment* indoors.
25. *kerosene*—We used a *kerosene* lamp.

GRADE 3

1. *pillow*—For a *pillow* Jacob had stones.
2. *number*—We cannot *number* the stars.
3. *kitten*—A *kitten* is a little cat.
4. *dollar*—A *dollar* equals one hundred cents.
5. *window*—Close the *window* when it is cold.
6. *umbrella*—Use the *umbrella* if it rains.
7. *can't*—I *can't* reach the high shelf.
8. *she'll*—Soon *she'll* get it for me.
9. *I'm*—Now *I'm* in the third grade.
10. *Mr.*—Does *Mr.* Martin own this store?
11. *Miss*—Will *Miss* Martin work here?
12. *Job*—We know *Job* was a patient man.
13. *John*—The apostle *John* followed Jesus.
14. *1 Peter*—Can you find *1 Peter* quickly?
15. *Jude*—The man *Jude* was a brother of Jesus.
16. *holy*—The Bible is a *holy* book.
17. *yourself*—Look at *yourself* in the mirror.
18. *windmill*—That *windmill* is very old.
19. *snowman*—The *snowman* melted fast.
20. *daylight*—Is it *daylight* outside?
21. *dirty*—We want to wash the *dirty* dishes.
22. *world*—God made the *world* and it was good.
23. *fur*—Animals have thick *fur* in winter.
24. *hurry*—When we *hurry* we make mistakes,
25. *earth*—Jesus came to *earth* as a baby.

GRADE 4

1. *remove*—For a time, David would not *remove* the ark of God.
2. *cents*—A man paid ten *cents* for an apple.
3. *mouse*—The cat caught a *mouse* for dinner.
4. *wooden*—Brooms have *wooden* handles.
5. *golden*—We gazed at the *golden* sunset.
6. *it's*—Yes, *it's* soon his birthday.
7. *unlike*—It is *unlike* him to be frowning.
8. *children*—Jesus loves the *children* dearly.
9. *twelve*—Jesus chose *twelve* disciples.
10. *easy*—"Knowledge is *easy* unto him that understandeth."
11. *space*—Not much *space* is left.
12. *mixed*—The cook *mixed* the sugar and flour.
13. *trunk*—Set the box into the *trunk,* please.
14. *careful*—Be *careful* as you spell.
15. *teeth*—We brush our *teeth* daily.
16. *chase*—Their turkey wanted to *chase* the chickens.
17. *awhile*—The baby slept *awhile* after dinner.
18. *pocketbook*—The girl's *pocketbook* is black.
19. *break*—Did the jar *break* when it fell?
20. *he'd*—We thought *he'd* be hurt.
21. *answer*—Say your *answer* loud and clear.
22. *music*—They learned a new song in *music* class.
23. *women*—Men, *women*, and children heard Ezra read.
24. *vacation*—Summer *vacation* will come soon.
25. *wisdom*—Jesus increased in *wisdom* and stature.

GRADE 7

1. *encourage*—Sugar will *encourage* ants.
2. *corporation*—Eight men formed a *corporation*.
3. *capitalization*—"I" receives *capitalization*.
4. *manual*—Shoveling is *manual* labor
5. *endeavor*—We want to help you in your *endeavor*.
6. *carnality*—Spirituality and *carnality* do not mix.
7. *corps*—A *corps* of rescue workers came to clean up.
8. *identify*—We can *identify* with Mary's joy.
9. *merchandise*—The *merchandise* sold well.
10. *Incarnation*—Jesus' *Incarnation* is a mystery.
11. *emphasize*—Underlining will *emphasize* the word.
12. *affiliate*—His store is an *affiliate* of a chain.
13. *patriarch*—An Indian chief was tribal *patriarch*.
14. *fiery*—Some *fiery* serpents bit the Israelites.
15. *difficulty*—A patient had *difficulty* breathing.
16. *patron*—Ken had long been a *patron* of that store.
17. *fraternity*—Many college boys join a *fraternity*.
18. *maternal*—She is our *maternal* grandmother.
19. *humility*—God values an attitude of calm *humility*.
20. *remedy*—Penicillin is a *remedy* for your sore throat.
21. *equine*—Mules and ponies are *equine* animals.
22. *canary*—Mother painted the kitchen a *canary* yellow.
23. *versatile*—A *versatile* man does many things well.
24. *cereal*—Farmers raise corn and other *cereal* grains.
25. *minor*—The old building contained some *minor* flaws.

GRADE 8

1. *testimony*—Stephen's *testimony* angered the crowd.
2. *violent*—He met a *violent* death.
3. *susceptible*—The righteous are *susceptible* to persecution.
4. *ornament*—Parental instruction is an *ornament* of grace.
5. *inhabitant*—Each *inhabitant* must pay tax.
6. *applicant*—He was an *applicant* for baptism.
7. *responsibility*—Privilege brings *responsibility*.
8. *solvent*—Love is a *solvent* for life's gritty irritants.
9. *tourist*—The new *tourist* center was perfect.
10. *architect*—A clever *architect* designed it to fit the scene.
11. *chauffeur*—Our grandparents should have a *chauffeur*.
12. *restaurant*—Judy bakes pies for a *restaurant* in town.
13. *employee*—She is the only *employee* who works at home.
14. *beige*—I lost my *beige* sweater.
15. *bouquet*—Put your *bouquet* on the bookshelf.
16. *camouflage*—It will *camouflage* the stained wallpaper.
17. *silhouette*—Could you identify everyone by his *silhouette*?
18. *revenue*—Income is reported to the *revenue* service.
19. *parliament*—The meeting resembled a *parliament* session.
20. *fatigue*—Orderly meetings cause less *fatigue*.
21. *adjourned*—The meeting *adjourned* in good time.
22. *flourish*—Some special flowers *flourish* in the desert.
23. *picturesque*—Spring is a very *picturesque* time.
24. *reservoir*—Memorized verses are a *reservoir* of inspiration.
25. *asterisk*—The *asterisk* guides you to some notes below.

LESSON

30

CONTINUED

GRADE 5

26. *zero*—The temperature was *zero* degrees.
27. *freeze*—Water will *freeze* when it is so cold.
28. *blaze*—The sunset made a glorious *blaze* in the west.
29. *resort*—Children *resort* to their parents for help.
30. *potatoes*—Peel enough *potatoes* for supper.
31. *escape*—Did your canary *escape* from its cage?
32. *burst*—The cherry trees *burst* into bloom.
33. *union*—Church members are a *union* working together.
34. *measles*—Three boys were sick with *measles*.
35. *except*—Everyone saw it *except* one girl.
36. *whisper*—I heard a *whisper* from the doorway.
37. *electric*—They use an *electric* heater.
38. *scarce*—Apricots were *scarce* this year.
39. *shouldn't*—I *shouldn't* forget to brush my teeth.
40. *hadn't*—The telephone *hadn't* rung all day.
41. *wreck*—The clothesline was a *wreck* after the storm.
42. *whether*—Who knows *whether* the seeds are covered?
43. *thieves*—No *thieves* will be in heaven.
44. *permitted*—Sunny days *permitted* outdoor games.
45. *they're*—Try some carrots because *they're* delicious.
46. *we've*—Yes, *we've* found the answer.
47. *yield*—One driver must *yield* the right-of-way.
48. *excitement*—In his *excitement* he forgot his address.
49. *sense*—The lady could *sense* that the child was scared.
50. *sword*—Jesus told Peter to put his *sword* away.

GRADE 6

26. *pickles*—These *pickles* are too sour.
27. *respectable*—He is a *respectable* person.
28. *occur*—When did your accident *occur*?
29. *yourselves*—You *yourselves* saw it happen.
30. *weapon*—A bird can use its beak as a *weapon*.
31. *court*—The basketball *court* was empty.
32. *expedition*—The *expedition* leaves tomorrow.
33. *elsewhere*—I was *elsewhere* at the time.
34. *watchful*—A *watchful* person is careful.
35. *accept*—Will you *accept* a suggestion?
36. *forwarding*—He left a *forwarding* address.
37. *excess*—The elephant weighed in *excess* of three tons.
38. *worthy*—John did not feel *worthy* to baptize Jesus.
39. *accident*—There was an *accident* last night.
40. *volume*—Find the *volume* of this cube.
41. *whatever*—I plan to be here *whatever* happens.
42. *universal*—Smiling is a *universal* expression.
43. *onion*—I like *onion* soup.
44. *accurate*—That was an *accurate* statement.
45. *beyond*—He worked *beyond* closing time.
46. *knowledge*—I had no *knowledge* of that.
47. *honesty*—*Honesty* helps friendships grow.
48. *companion*—Love is a *companion* to kindness.
49. *mg**—Medicine is measured in *milligrams*.
50. *Blvd.**—The *boulevard* south of town is being repaved.

GRADE 4

26. *Christmas*—December 25 is *Christm*as Day.
27. *reasons*—He wrote two *reasons* for the change.
28. *youngest*—Someone must be the *youngest* child.
29. *led*—One man *led* the way.
30. *gloves*—Are both your *gloves* wet?
31. *crossed*—The Israelites *crossed* the Jordan river.
32. *since*—Two months passed *since* it happened.
33. *dozen*—I purchased one *dozen* eggs.
34. *pictures*—Children like *pictures* of animals.
35. *silver*—Some men work in the *silver* mine.
36. *skates*—The ice *skates* are in the attic.
37. *carrying*—Mother cat is *carrying* her kitten.
38. *absent*—Several were *absent* that day.
39. *presents*—Some gave *presents* to the sick boy.
40. *checks*—Father writes *checks* to pay the bills.
41. *taught*—Jesus *taught* many people.
42. *unpainted*—Arnold bought an *unpainted* chair.
43. *praise*—I will *praise* the Lord.
44. *mercy*—"Surely goodness and *mercy* shall follow me."
45. *forgotten*—Has anyone *forgotten* anything?
46. *square*—Everything fit into the *square* box.
47. *we're*—I believe *we're* nearly finished.
48. *disorderly*—No one likes a *disorder*ly room.
49. *discolored*—Light *discolor*ed the curtains.
50. *whistle*—The engineer blew his *whistle* loud.

GRADE 7

26. *counsel*—Did you *counsel* with your parents?
27. *rite*—John first practiced the *rite* of Baptism.
28. *doubtless*—Do it, and you will *doubtless* succeed.
29. *feline*—Any *feline* animal eats meat.
30. *vaccine*—This *vaccine* will help resist the disease.
31. *senator*—A *senator* helps make laws.
32. *attached*—Baby Sue is *attached* to Mother.
33. *molecule*—The atoms joined to form a *molecule*.
34. *cassette*—Film for my camera comes in a *cassette*.
35. *schedule*—Did you *schedule* any time for reading?
36. *characters*—Two rough-looking *characters* came.
37. *senior*—My mother is thirty years my *senior*.
38. *dinette*—We ate lunch in a cozy *dinette*.
39. *rejuvenate*—Could you *rejuvenate* that old sofa?
40. *juvenile*—A *juvenile* may not sign the papers.
41. *occurrence*—Laws lessen the *occurrence* of fire.
42. *ancient*—The *ancient* Romans built sturdy roads.
43. *judgment*—God will bring *judgment* on all sin.
44. *argument*—Your *argument* is convincing.
45. *physician*—Ask a *physician* about an odd swelling.
46. *muscle*—The cardiac *muscle* never rests.
47. *courteous*—A *courteous* person wins many friends.
48. *temperature*—The *temperature* of water varies.
49. *mystery*—The fate of the Lost Colony is a *mystery*.
50. *descent*—Our neighbor is of Scottish *descent*.

GRADE 8

26. *maneuver*—It was hard to *maneuver* between the trees.
27. *galloped*—The herd *galloped* across the pasture.
28. *guaranteed*—This salve is *guaranteed* to relieve itching.
29. *anoint*—You should *anoint* the rash twice daily.
30. *fraud*—The peddler's *fraud* was exposed.
31. *pirate*—He tried to *pirate* his neighbor's poems.
32. *barbecue*—After the *barbecue*, the boys slept outside.
33. *ambitious*—They were *ambitious* about rigging up a tent.
34. *preparation*—It was dark before the *preparation* was done.
35. *coyote*—A yapping *coyote* startled them.
36. *resources*—Did they have *resources* for building a fence?
37. *voluntary*—There was plenty of *voluntary* labor.
38. *occasionally*—Jack *occasionally* gets a few spare bricks.
39. *continuously*—Water flows *continuously* over these falls.
40. *associated*—Waterfalls are *associated* with hydroelectricity.
41. *rheumatism*—Fido had *rheumatism* in his last years.
42. *canyon*—There is a clear echo in the *canyon*.
43. *meter*—The wind carried our velocity *meter* away.
44. *hurricane*—It was blowing with *hurricane* force.
45. *tornado*—A *tornado* is smaller but stronger.
46. *suicide*—It could be *suicide* to walk in its path.
47. *preference*—Which storm would be your *preference*?
48. *criticism*—Jesus had some *criticism* for the Pharisees.
49. *omitted*—They *omitted* the most important part of the Law.
50. *partial*—God does not accept *partial* obedience.

LESSON 31

1. *songs*—We sang two *songs* first of all.
2. *tests*—Our teacher gives *tests* to us.
3. *eyes*—He closed his *eyes* and slept.
4. *laws*—God gave *laws* to teach us how to live.
5. *yards*—The store clerk measured three *yards* of cloth.
6. *cards*—We send get-well *cards* to sick people.
7. *doors*—All the *doors* are shut.
8. *stores*—People shop at the *stores* in town.
9. *flies*—Many *flies* buzzed in the air.
10. *stars*—I like to look at the *stars* at night.
11. *dishes*—Put the clean *dishes* into the cupboard.
12. *wings*—Birds use their *wings* to fly.

*See Teacher's Manual for special instructions.

GRADE 5

1. *special*—Our parents are *special* to us.
2. *plantation*—The huge *plantation* raised much cotton.
3. *duties*—Do your *duties* with a smile.
4. *entertainment*—Too much *entertainment* is not good.
5. *sentence*—Write each *sentence* carefully.
6. *pattern*—The leaf *pattern* was unusual.
7. *profit*—We should *profit* from our mistakes.
8. *industry*—Growing *industry* helps the economy.
9. *salmon*—The school of *salmon* swam upstream.
10. *colonies*—In the lawn we saw two *colonies* of ants.
11. *limb*—The wind blew a *limb* off the tree.
12. *castle*—The children made a *castle* in the sand.
13. *mischief*—Nobody likes *mischief* makers.
14. *dumb*—A deaf and *dumb* person cannot hear or speak.
15. *hymn*—Paul and Silas sang a *hymn* of praise.
16. *prophet*—Daniel was a brave *prophet* of God.

Every *tablespoon* is bigger than a *teaspoon*.

This *pocketbook* belongs to someone from the *colony*.

GRADE 6

1. *effect*—What *effect* did this have on you?
2. *column*—Write the numbers in a straight *column*.
3. *amendment*—Congress passed a constitutional *amendment*.
4. *parable*—Do you know the *parable* of the lost sheep?
5. *iniquity*—The *iniquity* of Sodom was great.
6. *strength*—The Lord is my *strength* and shield.
7. *grammar*—Your *grammar* lesson is finished.
8. *practicing*—I am *practicing* this song.
9. *calendar*—The *calendar* says it is time for full moon.
10. *additional*—Do an *additional* lesson today.
11. *jealous*—God is a *jealous* God.
12. *advanced*—The old man was *advanced* in years.
13. *continued**—The story was *continued*.
14. *Song of Solomon**—*Song of Solomon* has beautiful poetry.
15. *Galatians**—*Galatians* 5 lists the fruit of the Spirit.
16. *Ephesians**—The armor of God is described in *Ephesians* 6.

He is the *governor* of an *industrial* state.

Saul's *fierce* anger had no *basis*.

GRADE 3

1. *park*—Father will *park* the car.
2. *crack*—Sunlight shone through the *crack* in the wall.
3. *tracks*—What animal *tracks* are those?
4. *queen*—Worker bees care for the *queen* bee.
5. *cave*—King Saul came into the *cave* where David was.
6. *thank*—One man remembered to *thank* Jesus.
7. *sticks*—The widow was gathering *sticks* to burn.
8. *kept*—Achan *kept* some things for himself.
9. *Christ*—Jesus *Christ* came to save sinners.
10. *arctic*—It is cold in the *arctic* region.
11. *picnic*—Not everyone has a *picnic* table.
12. *quick*—Father needed to make a *quick* decision.
13. *sack*—The *sack* is full of potatoes.
14. *cooked*—Mother *cooked* rice for supper.
15. *bark*—Deer rub the *bark* off some trees.
16. *corn*—Succotash is *corn* and lima beans.

GRADE 4

1. *flood*—During the *Flood,* Noah was safe.
2. *built*—Solomon *built* the first temple.
3. *beginning*—"In the *beginning* was the Word."
4. *enough*—The boy's lunch was *enough* for everyone.
5. *o'clock*—From four to six *o'clock* is two hours.
6. *building*—That high *building* is a skyscraper.
7. *geography*—We study land in *geography* class.
8. *elephant*—An African *elephant* has large ears.
9. *guess*—Is my *guess* right?
10. *handkerchief*— Fold a *handkerchief* neatly.
11. *laughed*—The baby *laughed* when she saw the toy.
12. *hungry*—We fed the *hungry* dog.
13. *calves*—Simon feeds the *calves* before breakfast.
14. *centimeter**—A pen is a *centimeter* thick.
15. *meter**—A *meter* stick is longer than a yardstick.
16. *kilometer**—A *kilometer* is a thousand meters.

I like to read *stories* of *heaven.*
Aren't any stars *shining*?

GRADE 7

1. *perceive*—Did you *perceive* a change in the clouds?
2. *salary*—The businessman was paid a high *salary.*
3. *conscience*—If we continue in sin, our *conscience* is dulled.
4. *aquarium*—We bought goldfish for our *aquarium.*
5. *performance*—A road test measures a driver's *performance.*
6. *transformed*—Peter was *transformed* into a different man.
7. *aqueduct*—Romans invented the *aqueduct* for water.
8. *conscious*—Reflexes take no *conscious* thought.
9. *permitted*—Revenge was *permitted* in olden times.
10. *export*—Petroleum is Saudi Arabia's chief *export.*
11. *translate*—Can you *translate* German into English?
12. *persistent*—A judge helped the *persistent* widow.
13. *import*—Our country must *import* coffee from Brazil.
14. *transparent*—We see through *transparent* glass.
15. *frequent*—A desert has *frequent* sandstorms.
16. *importunity*—Her *importunity* wearied the judge.
17. *persuade*—I did *persuade* Titus to climb the tower.
18. *transferred*—Amy *transferred* her seedlings.
19. *navigator*—The *navigator* had worked ten years.
20. *pertaining*—Nancy asked a question *pertaining* to grammar.
21. *transportation*—Cars are *transportation.*
22. *occupation*—Amos' *occupation* was herding sheep.
23. *pierce*—A balloon will burst if we *pierce* it.
24. *transgressions*—God forgives *transgressions.*
25. *opportunity*—Make friends at each *opportunity.*

GRADE 8

1. *communicate*—How did God *communicate* to Solomon?
2. *tender*—Two women claimed a *tender* child.
3. *responsible*—He was *responsible* to settle the dispute.
4. *satisfactorily*—His judgment answered it *satisfactorily.*
5. *unusually*—God gave him *unusually* great wisdom.
6. *plunder*—Piles of *plunder* filled the robbers' den.
7. *resolution*—The board passed a *resolution* about tardiness.
8. *kindergarten*—Children brought pets to *kindergarten.*
9. *poodle*—Jamie's *poodle* licked everyone's hands.
10. *aquarium*—Susan brought a little *aquarium* with goldfish.
11. *voyage*—The fish made a circling *voyage* all day.
12. *dachshund*—A sleepy *dachshund* lay on Maggie's sweater.
13. *salesman*—A kettle *salesman* came to our door.
14. *separately*—He would not sell his items *separately.*
15. *roommate*—Dale was my *roommate* for three years.
16. *university*—Now he is a *university* teacher.
17. *successor*—He is the *successor* of Mr. Turnbay.
18. *undoubtedly*—He has *undoubtedly* forgotten us.
19. *sauerkraut*—Will the *sauerkraut* cure in two weeks?
20. *refugees*—Where will the *refugees* stay?
21. *smallpox*—Some were afraid of the *smallpox* virus.
22. *supplement*—A vitamin *supplement* was given.
23. *trifle*—We should not *trifle* with health risks.
24. *sheer*—They sang for *sheer* delight.
25. *diesel*—Cold weather makes it harder to start a *diesel.*

LESSON 32

GRADE 2

1. *asked*—God *asked* Job many questions.
2. *carried*—Four men *carried* a sick man to Jesus.
3. *liked*—David *liked* to tend the sheep.
4. *loving*—We try to be *loving* and kind.
5. *passing*—The sun is *passing* behind a cloud.
6. *kicked*—The horse *kicked* up his heels.
7. *holding*—What is he *holding* in his hand?
8. *learned*—Have you *learned* your memory verse?
9. *riding*—The passengers are *riding* on the train.
10. *owned*—Mr. Smith *owned* the house before Mr. Hill did.
11. *burning*—The trash is *burning* rapidly.
12. *needed*—Mother *needed* sugar from the store.

*See Teacher's Manual for special instructions.

GRADE 5

1. *pitcher*—The taller *pitcher* contains milk.
2. *discovery*—The kitten *discovery* was thrilling.
3. *deacon*—Who is the *deacon* at your church?
4. *pupils*—All the *pupils* worked diligently.
5. *creature*—That *creature* looks like a lizard.
6. *awfully*—The girl was *awfully* sick.
7. *plainly*—How *plainly* do you talk?
8. *sleigh*—The *sleigh* glided over the snow.
9. *neither*—He could go *neither* forward nor backward.
10. *energy*—It takes *energy* to climb a hill.
11. *niece*—Mother's *niece* is my cousin.
12. *hymnal*—A *hymnal* is a book of hymns.
13. *deny*—Jesus knew Peter would *deny* Him thrice.
14. *Redeemer*—Our *Redeemer* is Jesus Christ.
15. *throne*—Jesus is at the *throne* of God.
16. *Holy Ghost*—The *Holy Ghost* came upon them.
　　Grandma's youngest sister lives far away.
　　The *boy's* aunt sends him pretty cards from the *island*.

GRADE 6

1. *education*—Our *education* includes everything that we learn.
2. *arrival*—We had a new *arrival* today.
3. *valuable*—Time is too *valuable* to waste.
4. *honorable*—You must do the *honorable* thing.
5. *mirror*—He looked in the *mirror*.
6. *estimate*—*Estimate* your answer before computing it.
7. *community*—That is a *community* park.
8. *immediately*—He left *immediately* afterward.
9. *scenery*—The *scenery* is beautiful.
10. *society*—In our *society*, the handshake is a common greeting.
11. *quotation*—Romans 3:12 is a *quotation* from Psalms.
12. *humanity*—Christ's *humanity* is plainly taught in the Bible.
13. *destination*—Their *destination* was the South Pole.
14. *believing*—Faith means *believing* without seeing.
15. *data*—Satellites collect *data* about the weather.
16. *description*—Give me a *description* of him.
　　This *museum* is *beautifully* built.
　　The *deliveries* will soon *approach* fifty.

GRADE 3

1. *school*—After *school* we do our chores.
2. *quarter*—The boy gave a *quarter* for his offering.
3. *sixty*—The neighbor lady was *sixty* years old.
4. *tank*—The milk *tank* is full.
5. *next*—You may be *next* in line.
6. *sky*—White clouds in a blue *sky* are beautiful.
7. *books*—How many *books* did you borrow?
8. *cart*—The man's *cart* needs a new tire.
9. *fixed*—The broken window is *fixed* now.
10. *calf*—How fast the little *calf* is growing!
11. *ax*—The man used an *ax* to split wood.
12. *rocks*—Some fields have many *rocks* in them.
13. *bucket*—A full *bucket* of water is heavy.
14. *Christ*—Jesus *Christ* is the Son of God.
15. *quick*—Mother stirred the batter with *quick* strokes.
16. *thank*—Remember to *thank* the man for his help.

GRADE 4

1. *sleepy*—When I am *sleepy*, I cannot work well.
2. *bicycle*—Roger must pump up the *bicycle* tire.
3. *juice*—Orange *juice* is good to drink.
4. *fields*—Many *fields* were planted by hand in Bible times.
5. *owner*—Who is the *owner* of this lunch box?
6. *beautiful*—Adam and Eve saw *beautiful* fruit.
7. *suit*—Yes, it will *suit* us to make sandwiches.
8. *peas*—We often eat *peas* and carrots mixed.
9. *fruit*—How many *fruit* trees are in his orchard?
10. *believe*—We *believe* that Jesus rose again.
11. *chief*—The *chief* butler forgot about Joseph.
12. *received*—"Freely ye have *received*, freely give."
13. *suddenly*—Light *suddenly* shone in the prison.
14. *liter**—One *liter* is ten deciliters.
15. *gram**—One *gram* is ten decigrams.
16. *kilogram**—One *kilogram* is a thousand grams.

The *greatest* need cannot wait until *later*.

Is your *piece* of paper *thinner* than his?

GRADE 7

1. *accidentally*—He *accidentally* spilled milk.
2. *occasion*—On one *occasion*, Jesus healed ten lepers.
3. *surrender*—We must *surrender* to Christ as Lord.
4. *intercede*—Jonathan did *intercede* for David.
5. *oxygen*—A fire needs fuel and *oxygen* to burn.
6. *surrounded*—The village was *surrounded* by hills.
7. *awkward*—David did not wear Saul's *awkward* armor.
8. *precisely*—We arrived *precisely* at seven o'clock.
9. *scissors*—Doctors use *scissors* to snip stitches.
10. *dissect*—Students *dissect* animals to study them.
11. *superficial*—His accident wounds are only *superficial*.
12. *ultimate*—Serving Jesus brings the *ultimate* joy.
13. *fungicide*—A *fungicide* spray can stop plant rust.
14. *superlative*—Only God has *superlative* wisdom.
15. *succeed*—Who will *succeed* your schoolteacher then?
16. *genuine*—Carl's shoes are made of *genuine* leather.
17. *superscription*—Read the *superscription* on a dime.
18. *ultraviolet*—We cannot see *ultraviolet* rays.
19. *herbicide*—He sprinkled *herbicide* on the weeds.
20. *supersede*—Heaven will *supersede* all glory here.
21. *advise*—Doctors *advise* us to watch our salt intake.
22. *incident*—He told the *incident* of killing a bear.
23. *superstition*—We disbelieve all *superstition*.
24. *wrought*—God *wrought* miracles to free the Israelites.
25. *insecticide*—Will the *insecticide* also kill helpful insects?

GRADE 8

1. *opportunities*—Make good use of *opportunities*.
2. *arrangements*—We practiced new music *arrangements*.
3. *soprano*—Connie often sings *soprano*.
4. *alto*—She will practice *alto* today.
5. *bass*—We need a strong *bass* singer.
6. *zero*—Begin with *zero* at the bottom of your graph.
7. *sergeant*—An army *sergeant* visited the orchard.
8. *sufficiently*—Some apples were *sufficiently* ripe to sample.
9. *shouted*—The farmer *shouted* at the strangers.
10. *tenor*—Suddenly the *tenor* of their visit changed.
11. *peaceable*—They parted on *peaceable* terms.
12. *penicillin*—A British scientist discovered *penicillin* in 1928.
13. *buffalo*—Indians made many things from *buffalo* materials.
14. *artificial*—Today we use *artificial* products.
15. *crescendo*—The singers' voices rose to a *crescendo*.
16. *skiing*—Watch the water bugs *skiing* on a puddle.
17. *limestone*—Sit on the *limestone* wall and dream a bit.
18. *volcano*—A roaring *volcano* spewed fire and lava.
19. *temporary*—There was *temporary* panic in the city.
20. *unbeliever*—Such an event makes an *unbeliever* tremble.
21. *so-called*—Many *so-called* Christians also turned to God.
22. *repentance*—God longs for the *repentance* of every sinner.
23. *indefinitely*—The bridge was closed *indefinitely*.
24. *serial*—A new *serial* begins in this issue.
25. *motto*—Each story is based on the *motto* of a famous person.

LESSON 33

GRADE 2

1. *storm*—There was a great *storm* last week.
2. *into*—Noah went *into* the ark.
3. *upon*—The sacrifice was laid *upon* the altar.
4. *many*—Jesus healed *many* people.
5. *water*—Rebekah got *water* for the camels to drink.
6. *hands*—I have two *hands* to work for Jesus.
7. *filling*—The man is *filling* the oil tank.
8. *river*—We crossed the *river* on a bridge.
9. *zoo*—At the *zoo* we saw giraffes.
10. *ring*—Will the bell *ring* soon?
11. *pony*—The *pony* eats grass in the pasture.
12. *carries*—The postman *carries* a big bag.

*See Teacher's Manual for special instructions.

GRADE 5

1. *declare*—"The heavens *declare* the glory of God."
2. *appeared*—Paul *appeared* before King Agrippa.
3. *decide*—Always *decide* to do the right.
4. *suppose*—I *suppose* you enjoyed that book.
5. *satisfied*—Are you *satisfied* with that color?
6. *tardy*—The girls were *tardy* for school.
7. *let's*—Come, *let's* go in.
8. *bury*—We must *bury* the seed so that it can grow.
9. *frightened*—The siren *frightened* the cows.
10. *grabbed*—Frisky *grabbed* the shoe and ran.
11. *pronounce*—Do you *pronounce* your words clearly?
12. *attended*—A large group *attended* the service.
13. *guide*—Some blind people have dogs to *guide* them.
14. *weren't*—No, the boys *weren't* outside.
15. *automobile*—Our *automobile* is in the garage.
16. *alligators*—The *alligators* have strong jaws.

Look *tomorrow* to see if the Bible is on the *pulpit*.
Their *daughter* told us to *rejoice* because they were well.

GRADE 6

1. *eternity*—The length of *eternity* is awesome.
2. *auditorium*—The *auditorium* was cleaned.
3. *gnawing*—There was a *gnawing* sound in the wall.
4. *expression*—Read with *expression* and meaning.
5. *vary*—Your answers will *vary* greatly.
6. *afford*—Can you *afford* to lose?
7. *enforce*—Policemen must *enforce* the law.
8. *announcement*—Make the *announcement* today.
9. *transfer*—You may *transfer* to the other bus.
10. *discontinued*—That service has been *discontinued*.
11. *whence*—You cannot see *whence* it cometh.
12. *moderate*—There was a *moderate* rise in temperature.
13. *godliness*—"*Godliness* with contentment is great gain."
14. *happiness*—Joy and *happiness* are not the same.
15. *connection*—This *connection* seems loose.
16. *constantly*—He is *constantly* helping someone.

I was *disappointed* by the *bulletin*.
The *bough* crushed the *currant* bush.

78

GRADE 3

1. *stood*—Ezra *stood* on a pulpit of wood.
2. *could*—The people *could* hear what Ezra said.
3. *truth*—Speak the *truth* always.
4. *tomb*—Lazarus had been in the *tomb* four days.
5. *grew*—Our garden *grew* well last year.
6. *boots*—Wear your *boots* if the grass is wet.
7. *bushel*—We dug a *bushel* of potatoes.
8. *wolf*—Have you ever heard a *wolf* howl?
9. *would*—That plan *would* suit very well.
10. *tooth*—The *tooth* hurt because it had a cavity.
11. *flew*—A bluebird *flew* from its nest.
12. *true*—Is that story a *true* happening?
13. *move*—Please *move* forward a little.
14. *books*—Boxes of *books* are heavy.
15. *quarter*—Mother paid a *quarter* for the carrots.
16. *school*—Our *school* year is nearly ended.

GRADE 4

1. *curve*—The road makes a *curve* around the hill.
2. *great-uncle*—My *great-uncle* makes chairs.
3. *poem*—A *poem* is written by a poet.
4. *cookbook*—Which *cookbook* has the recipe?
5. *tomorrow*—God will care for us *tomorrow* too.
6. *downstairs*—We went *downstairs* quietly.
7. *good-bye*—Rhoda waved *good-bye* from the window.
8. *great-grandmother*—She is my *great-grandmother*.
9. *terrible*—Some lands had a *terrible* famine.
10. *mountains*—How many *mountains* can you name?
11. *against*—Prop the ladder *against* the house.
12. *pint**—One *pint* equals two cups.
13. *quart**—One *quart* equals two pints.
14. *ounce**—An *ounce* of water is about two tablespoons.
15. *gallon**—One *gallon* equals four quarts.
16. *pound**—One *pound* is sixteen ounces.

Those *pictures* may *scare* Ezra.
The men were *painting* the *Mennonite* church.

GRADE 7

1. *restrain*—Andrew tried to *restrain* the horses.
2. *discipline*—We need to *discipline* ourselves.
3. *betray*—A true friend will not *betray* our trust.
4. *receiver*—Listen to the voice in the telephone *receiver*.
5. *extremely*—It is *extremely* warm at the equator.
6. *secede*—Several states did *secede* from the Union.
7. *exception*—Is there any *exception* to the rule?
8. *cafeteria*—I ate lunch in the hospital *cafeteria*.
9. *gradually*—The air *gradually* fades into space.
10. *legislation*—The new *legislation* takes effect immediately.
11. *rectify*—Some problems are difficult to *rectify*.
12. *captivate*—The puppy seemed to *captivate* us.
13. *selection*—They offer a good *selection* of shoes.
14. *legitimate*—Do not overdo a *legitimate* activity.
15. *regiment*—Some governments *regiment* a citizen's life.
16. *cashier*—Mother paid the *cashier* for the groceries.
17. *mandate*—Did the king's *mandate* stop Daniel's prayers?
18. *cassette*—Norman recorded with a *cassette* player.
19. *commander*—The army's chief *commander* is the president.
20. *mandatory*—Elementary school is *mandatory*.
21. *regulator*—Is this a *regulator* for the furnace?
22. *delegate*—Good leaders *delegate* tasks to others.
23. *receipts*—Stores compute total *receipts* daily.
24. *correction*—We all need *correction* at times.
25. *pamphlet*—Read the *pamphlet* about highway safety.

GRADE 8

1. *identify*—How did Adam *identify* all the animals?
2. *jaguar*—The *jaguar* was tame in the beginning.
3. *caribou*—The *caribou* is a large deer.
4. *llama*—A *llama* is useful for mountain travel.
5. *opossum*—Nighttime is when the *opossum* roams.
6. *raccoon*—The *raccoon* also hunts at night.
7. *classify*—We *classify* animals by structure.
8. *tomahawk*—Was the *tomahawk* used in hunting?
9. *tapioca*—Cassava roots yield *tapioca*.
10. *chocolate*—Cacao beans produce *chocolate*.
11. *utilize*—Can they *utilize* the dry hulls?
12. *tobacco*—Some value is found in *tobacco*.
13. *justify*—Does that *justify* raising the crop?
14. *sanctify*—We cannot *sanctify* harmful habits.
15. *realize*—Most people *realize* the harm of nicotine.
16. *canoe*—See the brown *canoe* on the beach.
17. *moccasin*—A water *moccasin* was hiding beneath it.
18. *prophesy*—Which city did Jonah *prophesy* against?
19. *emphasize*—Their actions *emphasize* their repentance.
20. *spiritualize*—The Indians *spiritualize* their harvest.
21. *simplify*—Plain obedience will *simplify* life.
22. *reign*—God's *reign* is eternal.
23. *pressurize*—Don't *pressurize* the balloon too much.
24. *tying*—We are *tying* up the loose ends.
25. *itemize*—Then we can *itemize* our summer plans.

LESSON 34

*See Teacher's Manual for special instructions.

GRADE 2

1. *stars*—How bright the *stars* are shining!
2. *doors*—Close all the *doors* and windows.
3. *eyes*—The bright light made my *eyes* hurt.
4. *songs*—We know many *songs* by memory.
5. *dishes*—Wash the *dishes* carefully.
6. *flies*—An airplane *flies* high in the sky.
7. *wings*—The eagle lifted its *wings* and soared away.
8. *cards*—We send get-well *cards* to sick people.
9. *holding*—The conductor is *holding* all the tickets.
10. *burning*—Father is *burning* trash today.
11. *needed*—No one *needed* more time.
12. *asked*—Charles *asked* for the green crayon.
13. *riding*—We like to go *riding* in the car.
14. *liked*—All of us *liked* that story.
15. *carried*—The boy *carried* our groceries to the car.
16. *passing*—The day is *passing* rapidly.
17. *into*—Step *into* your boots.
18. *storm*—During the *storm* big trees blew over.
19. *upon*—Jesus rode *upon* a donkey.
20. *hands*—"Work with your own *hands*" is a Bible verse.
21. *water*—We need *water* to wash our clothes.
22. *many*—How *many* kinds do you have?
23. *filling*—We are *filling* the jugs with milk.
24. *carries*—The postman *carries* the mail.
25. *river*—Water flooded the *river* bank.

GRADE 5

1. *suppose*—Do you *suppose* that the plant will bloom?
2. *pattern*—Mother cut around the *pattern* carefully.
3. *plainly*—We heard the bell *plainly* from outside.
4. *bury*—Watch the dog *bury* his bone.
5. *awfully*—The poor horse limped *awfully*.
6. *attended*—Our minister *attended* the meeting.
7. *sentence*—Read the next *sentence*, please.
8. *satisfied*—Yes, we are *satisfied* with that.
9. *hymnal*—Open your *hymnal* to number 1.
10. *profit*—Would a sharper blade *profit* you any?
11. *entertainment*—A good book is enjoyable *entertainment*.
12. *appeared*—The moon *appeared* from behind a tree.
13. *discovery*—I just made an important *discovery*.
14. *special*—Sunday is a *special* day.
15. *declare*—"The heavens *declare* the glory of God."
16. *plantation*—A rich man owned the huge *plantation*.
17. *niece*—The old lady's *niece* cares for her.
18. *Redeemer*—Christ our *Redeemer* died on the cross.
19. *decide*—We could *decide* that later.
20. *castle*—The ruins of the *castle* stand on the hill.
21. *guide*—The Bible is our *guide* through life.
22. *duties*—Many *duties* wait to be done.
23. *Holy Ghost*—The *Holy Ghost* lives in Christians' hearts.
24. *tardy*—No one likes to be *tardy* for school.
25. *salmon*—The *salmon* swim upstream every year.

GRADE 6

1. *effect*—The medicine had a bad *effect* on his heart.
2. *amendment*—Delete that last *amendment*.
3. *grammar*—We will not have a *grammar* lesson today.
4. *column*—He stood by a *column* of the old building.
5. *practicing*—I am *practicing* my penmanship.
6. *education*—A good *education* is important.
7. *parable*—Hear the *parable* of the sower.
8. *advanced*—He *advanced* by one step.
9. *iniquity*—God hates *iniquity*.
10. *calendar*—That *calendar* still shows March.
11. *Ephesians*—The Book of *Ephesians* is a letter.
12. *strength*—Samson had no *strength* left.
13. *additional*—I will give you an *additional* test.
14. *Song of Solomon*—*Song of Solomon* follows Ecclesiastes.
15. *valuable*—You are wasting *valuable* time.
16. *jealous*—Saul was *jealous* of David.
17. *Galatians*—*Galatians* tells of a special fruit.
18. *immediately*—Pam left *immediately*.
19. *arrival*—We waited for the *arrival* of the bus.
20. *community*—This *community* is new to me.
21. *scenery*—I watched the *scenery* from the window.
22. *honorable*—Joseph was an *honorable* person.
23. *mirror*—Please wipe the *mirror* for me.
24. *society*—Ants have a well-ordered *society*.
25. *estimate*—He will *estimate* the pig's weight.

GRADE 3

1. *kept*—Have you *kept* your paper neat?
2. *thank*—We should *thank* God for His love.
3. *crack*—We will *crack* the walnuts soon.
4. *tracks*—Who made these *tracks* in the snow?
5. *picnic*—We had a *picnic* for lunch.
6. *arctic*—It is cold in the *arctic* region.
7. *Christ*—Jesus *Christ* blessed the children.
8. *books*—How many *books* are in your desk?
9. *tank*—There was a big *tank* in the barn.
10. *calf*—You may feed the new *calf* tonight.
11. *bucket*—It drinks from a *bucket* now.
12. *school*—We will go to *school* today.
13. *quarter*—A *quarter* is twenty-five cents.
14. *sixty*—Are there *sixty* students here?
15. *next*—Karen sat *next* to me at the table.
16. *stood*—We *stood* to sing this morning.
17. *could*—We *could* have extra drill today.
18. *wolf*—A *wolf* is a fierce animal.
19. *bushel*—The *bushel* basket is full.
20. *tooth*—Did you lose a *tooth* lately?
21. *truth*—Tell the *truth* at all times.
22. *grew*—Tom *grew* one inch since last year.
23. *tomb*—In a new *tomb* they buried Jesus.
24. *true*—It is *true* that God loves you.
25. *move*—We will *move* to a new house.

GRADE 4

1. *cookbook*—Which *cookbook* has the salad recipe?
2. *good-bye*—The boys waved *good-bye* a long time.
3. *o'clock*—A whistle blew at twelve *o'clock* noon.
4. *pound*—"Thy *pound* hath gained ten pounds."
5. *great-uncle*—Is your *great-uncle* living?
6. *suit*—Jesus' teachings did not *suit* the Pharisees.
7. *downstairs*—She tiptoed *downstairs* quietly.
8. *fruit*—"A good tree bringeth forth good *fruit*."
9. *peas*—We like *peas* with browned butter.
10. *sleepy*—Who is *sleepy* today?
11. *guess*—No one could *guess* the name.
12. *chief*—Columbus is a *chief* city in Ohio.
13. *laughed*—Sarah *laughed* at the angel's message.
14. *ounce*—This bottle holds half an *ounce* of glue.
15. *beautiful*—Spring is a *beautiful* season.
16. *fields*—Wheat *fields* are turning green.
17. *curve*—The path makes a *curve* around the rock.
18. *mountains*—Those *mountains* have snow on them.
19. *against*—Do not lean *against* the car.
20. *calves*—Three *calves* stood beside the fence.
21. *suddenly*—The engine *suddenly* stopped running.
22. *built*—Solomon *built* the temple.
23. *building*—What a magnificent *building* it was!
24. *hungry*—Jesus fed the *hungry* multitude.
25. *quart*—Only one *quart* of oil is left.

GRADE 7

1. *performance*—Rest aids *performance*.
2. *aquarium*—At the zoo *aquarium*, we fed a dolphin.
3. *permitted*—The weather *permitted* early plowing.
4. *aqueduct*—An *aqueduct* carries water.
5. *persistent*—Ray's *persistent* earache went away.
6. *export*—Does our country *export* wheat to Russia?
7. *pertaining*—Here are x-rays *pertaining* to teeth.
8. *importunity*—Her *importunity* brought justice.
9. *pierce*—Use this instrument to *pierce* the can.
10. *navigator*—The *navigator* sailed to Spain.
11. *salary*—Some workers are paid a fixed *salary*.
12. *occupation*—We enjoy the *occupation* of our home.
13. *translate*—Friends *translate* words into actions.
14. *opportunity*—Wait for an *opportunity* to speak.
15. *transparent*—Most glass is *transparent*.
16. *perceive*—Jesus could *perceive* hidden thoughts.
17. *transportation*—Air *transportation* ceased.
18. *oxygen*—The element *oxygen* is plentiful.
19. *accidentally*—Inventions do come *accidentally*.
20. *supersede*—New leaders *supersede* present ones.
21. *awkward*—Lucy felt *awkward* and shy.
22. *precisely*—You said *precisely* what I thought.
23. *dissect*—The scientist will *dissect* the odd plant.
24. *superstition*—Faith opposes all *superstition*.
25. *genuine*—John would baptize only *genuine* believers.

GRADE 8

1. *responsible*—You are *responsible* for great influence.
2. *separately*—Wash dark clothes *separately* from white.
3. *diesel*—The old *diesel* gave good service.
4. *satisfactorily*—The loose shingle was *satisfactorily* nailed.
5. *refugees*—Flood *refugees* crowded the school.
6. *plunder*—All their *plunder* was swept downstream.
7. *trifle*—Open the window a *trifle*.
8. *unusually*—The wind is *unusually* cold.
9. *tender*—What spoiled the *tender* grapes?
10. *undoubtedly*—It was *undoubtedly* some little foxes.
11. *resolution*—We need fresh *resolution* to keep them out.
12. *successor*—The captain's *successor* painted his ship.
13. *sauerkraut*—He always has *sauerkraut* with his sausage.
14. *poodle*—The clipped *poodle* looked much different.
15. *university*—We visited the *university* library.
16. *supplement*—I got two books to *supplement* my study.
17. *sheer*—The hillside is too *sheer* for mowing.
18. *arrangements*—Flight *arrangements* should be made early.
19. *opportunities*—Make the most of your *opportunities*.
20. *sufficiently*—Is the paint *sufficiently* dry?
21. *alto*—Karen memorized her *alto* music.
22. *tenor*—She sang a duet with the *tenor* part.
23. *temporary*—There will be a *temporary* detour.
24. *indefinitely*—We may use the garden *indefinitely*.
25. *limestone*—Add *limestone* dust to improve the soil.

LESSON 34
CONTINUED

*See Teacher's Manual for special instructions.

GRADE 5

26. *deny*—A Christian must *deny* himself.
27. *industry*—Cities are centers of *industry* and business.
28. *hymn*—Choose a *hymn* for us to sing.
29. *automobile*—This store sells *automobile* tires.
30. *energy*—Sunlight is a form of *energy*.
31. *pronounce*—The minister will *pronounce* the benediction.
32. *limb*—A tree *limb* broke in the storm.
33. *deacon*—A *deacon* loves to help the church.
34. *grabbed*—The little boy *grabbed* his coat.
35. *sleigh*—An old *sleigh* is in the barn.
36. *pitcher*—Fill the *pitcher* with water.
37. *mischief*—Those goats are always in *mischief*.
38. *alligators*—Don't *alligators* live in warm climates?
39. *dumb*—Animals are *dumb* because they cannot speak.
40. *prophet*—Malachi was a *prophet* of God.
41. *let's*—After supper *let's* weed the garden.
42. *throne*—God sees us from His *throne* each day.
43. *colonies*—Thirteen *colonies* united as a nation.
44. *neither*—"Give me *neither* poverty nor riches."
45. *weren't*—The calves *weren't* finished eating.
46. *creature*—A fuzzy *creature* crawled up my arm.
47. *frightened*—That noise *frightened* me.
48. *pupils*—All the *pupils* finished the test.

GRADE 6

26. *quotation*—That *quotation* is from Genesis.
27. *humanity*—We believe in Christ's *humanity*.
28. *believing*—The Israelites were *believing* a lie.
29. *destination*—Our *destination* is the same.
30. *eternity*—*Eternity* is immeasurable.
31. *data*—The scientist collected *data* about insects.
32. *discontinued*—His paper was *discontinued*.
33. *description*—Your *description* was helpful.
34. *vary*—Your answers may *vary* greatly.
35. *auditorium*—The *auditorium* was soon full.
36. *gnawing*—A rodent is a *gnawing* animal.
37. *constantly*—She was *constantly* helping.
38. *expression*—Do not use that *expression*.
39. *afford*—We cannot *afford* to become lazy.
40. *godliness*—*Godliness* includes many virtues.
41. *moderate*—The boy ate a *moderate* lunch.
42. *enforce*—The policeman must *enforce* the law.
43. *announcement*—I read the *announcement*.
44. *whence*—From *whence* did they come?
45. *connection*—This *connection* is loose.
46. *happiness*—Your *happiness* is important to me.
47. *continued*—The story is *continued* on page 34.
48. *transfer*—The bank agreed to *transfer* the money.
49. *Eph.**—*Ephesians* follows Galatians.
50. *cont.**—The story was *continued* on page 50.

GRADE 4

26. *owner*—The *owner* has the key.
27. *gallon*—Mother bought a *gallon* of milk.
28. *tomorrow*—Tonight or *tomorrow* it may rain.
29. *enough*—One pie is *enough* for dinner.
30. *flood*—Noah's family was saved from the *Flood*.
31. *poem*—The teacher read a *poem* about diligence.
32. *geography*—Have you studied Bible lands *geography*?
33. *beginning*—Read the *beginning* of the story.
34. *received*—We have *received* many blessings.
35. *bicycle*—Someone left his *bicycle* outside.
36. *pint*—The recipe calls for a *pint* of cream.
37. *kilogram*—The box holds a *kilogram* of rice.
38. *gram*—One *gram* of water is not very heavy.
39. *liter*—This bottle holds a *liter* of milk.
40. *kilometer*—Sally walks a *kilometer* to church.
41. *meter*—Mother bought a *meter* of apron material.
42. *lb.**—Sixteen ounces are in a *pound*.
43. *gal.**—Four quarts are in a *gallon*.
44. *oz.**—A pound is more than an *ounce*.
45. *qt.**—A gallon is more than a *quart*.
46. *g**—Two paper clips weigh one *gram*.
47. *l**—Gasoline is measured by the *liter*.
48. *cm**—A large paper clip is one *centimeter* wide.
49. *m**—Four books laid end to end measure one *meter*.
50. *km**—Distance between cities is measured in *kilometers*.

GRADE 7

26. *herbicide*—Will this *herbicide* harm any wildlife?
27. *superficial*—He had only *superficial* friends.
28. *surrender*—A defeated army must then *surrender*.
29. *ultraviolet*—The *ultraviolet* rays cause a tan.
30. *insecticide*—An *insecticide* fights mosquitoes.
31. *surrounded*—An island is *surrounded* by water.
32. *occasion*—Pilate had no *occasion* to condemn Jesus.
33. *superscription*—I can read a *superscription*.
34. *ultimate*—Our God is the *ultimate* authority.
35. *discipline*—Learning to type takes *discipline*.
36. *betray*—Our face will often *betray* our thoughts.
37. *rectify*—Andy quickly tried to *rectify* his mistake.
38. *cafeteria*—The *cafeteria* offered Chinese food.
39. *exception*—They took *exception* to Christ's healings.
40. *captivate*—Bright colors *captivate* a small child.
41. *receipts*—Two sales *receipts* could not be found.
42. *restrain*—Eli did not *restrain* his wicked sons.
43. *cashier*—The *cashier* calculated the total bill.
44. *legitimate*—Eric's absence was *legitimate*.
45. *secede*—Poor health forced him to *secede* from them.
46. *commander*—Joab was David's *commander*.
47. *mandatory*—Is seat belt use *mandatory* here?
48. *regulator*—A faulty *regulator* makes a clock lose time.
49. *delegate*—Our state sent a *delegate* to a meeting.
50. *selection*—His *selection* of a drill took time.

GRADE 8

26. *serial*—Janet is writing a *serial* about pioneers.
27. *peaceable*—Indians were *peaceable* with some.
28. *volcano*—They thought the *volcano* was God's wrath.
29. *soprano*—There was a prominent *soprano* voice.
30. *crescendo*—It rang out in the *crescendo*.
31. *shouted*—Terry *shouted* above the noise.
32. *motto*—A *motto* is a good reminder.
33. *repentance*—John preached *repentance*.
34. *penicillin*—Alexander Fleming discovered *penicillin*.
35. *raccoon*—We caught a *raccoon* in the corn patch.
36. *classify*—Would you *classify* him as a robber?
37. *realize*—Now we *realize* what damaged the corn.
38. *spiritualize*—We can *spiritualize* our work.
39. *sanctify*—Singing helps to *sanctify* our hearts.
40. *reign*—Jesus will not *reign* in a defiled heart.
41. *pressurize*—They must *pressurize* highflying jets.
42. *moccasin*—There is a hole in Alma's *moccasin*.
43. *caribou*—Here is a piece of *caribou* leather.
44. *utilize*—See if you can *utilize* it for a patch.
45. *simplify*—Let's *simplify* the supper plans.
46. *itemize*—Will you *itemize* the menu?
47. *tapioca*—Jane will bring *tapioca* pudding.
48. *llama*—Pedro led his *llama* to market.
49. *tying*—He was *tying* it when the load fell off.
50. *tobacco*—Keep the air clear of *tobacco* smoke.

GRADE 2

1. *rain*—See how fast the *rain* is falling.
2. *his*—The man ate *his* lunch under the tree.
3. *hill*—Climbing the steep *hill* made us puff.
4. *road*—Beside the *road* were some pretty flowers.
5. *sleep*—Children need many hours of *sleep* at night.
6. *head*—Bring in a *head* of lettuce.
7. *thing*—What is that *thing* on the ceiling?
8. *catch*—I could hardly *catch* the ball.
9. *milk*—People use *milk* to make cheese.
10. *made*—Mother *made* four pies.
11. *mail*—We send *mail* at the post office.
12. *eye*—Close your right *eye* a bit.
13. *shoe*—Did you find your other *shoe* yet?
14. *helps*—This salve *helps* to stop the itching.
15. *first*—Sweep the floor *first* of all.
16. *back*—"Come *back* again," they said.
17. *place*—You may *place* your things on the table.
18. *when*—Read clearly *when* your turn comes.
19. *highest*—What was the *highest* temperature yesterday?
20. *apples*—Those red *apples* are delicious.
21. *dishes*—I will wash the *dishes* now.
22. *asked*—God *asked* Job many questions.
23. *water*—The *water* in the lake looked blue.
24. *worked*—He sang as he *worked* all day.
25. *singing*—The boys and girls are *singing* happily.

GRADE 5

1. *solid*—"On Christ, the *solid* Rock, I stand."
2. *sandwich*—Make a cheese *sandwich* to eat.
3. *linger*—The dewdrops could not *linger* long.
4. *motion*—Watch for the usher to *motion* to us.
5. *junk*—Add this to the *junk* pile.
6. *writing*—The pupils are *writing* neatly.
7. *February*—After January come *February* and March.
8. *dairy*—People buy milk at the *dairy* store.
9. *shovel*—Someone should *shovel* the walk open.
10. *valley*—A fertile *valley* is between the mountains.
11. *twenty-five*—A quarter is *twenty-five* cents.
12. *strain*—I needed to *strain* my ears to hear.
13. *hero*—The Israelites honored David as a *hero*.
14. *salmon*—Mother prepared *salmon* for dinner.
15. *careless*—The *careless* boy lost his shoes.
16. *energy*—Are you full of *energy* today?
17. *view*—What a lovely *view* of the mountains.
18. *deacon*—Our *deacon* dismissed the meeting.
19. *invention*—What a handy *invention* a can opener is.
20. *neither*—The sick girl *neither* ate nor slept.
21. *beauty*—We drank in the *beauty* of the sunrise.
22. *thought*—No one *thought* to bring spoons.
23. *warehouse*—A huge *warehouse* is beside the ship.
24. *collect*—Spoutings *collect* rain from roofs.
25. *collar*—A new shirt *collar* is stiff.

GRADE 6

1. *copies*—Give two *copies* to your father.
2. *tithe*—A *tithe* is a tenth.
3. *oyster*—Lester's mother made *oyster* stew.
4. *congress*—A *congress* makes new laws.
5. *invoice*—That pink paper is the *invoice*.
6. *tongue*—Christ's love is more than *tongue* can tell.
7. *chorus*—We sang the *chorus* softly.
8. *paragraph*—Indent each new *paragraph*.
9. *wrestle*—Do not *wrestle* your problems alone.
10. *attack*—Do not make an *attack* on his character.
11. *automatic*—The plane has an *automatic* pilot.
12. *pigeon*—There is a *pigeon* in the barn.
13. *electrical*—An *electrical* storm lit up the sky.
14. *bureau*—The *bureau* had four drawers.
15. *syllable*—Pronounce each *syllable* distinctly.
16. *everlasting*—He is the *everlasting* God.
17. *believed*—The disciples *believed* and rejoiced.
18. *principle*—Daniel was a man of *principle*.
19. *reindeer*—Are there *reindeer* in America?
20. *deceive*—We cannot *deceive* God.
21. *surface*—On the *surface*, things seemed normal.
22. *reverse*—His actions were the *reverse* of his words.
23. *international*—All nations are to obey *international* laws.
24. *debtor*—Paul was *debtor* to both Jews and Gentiles.
25. *dispatch*—I want to *dispatch* a telegram.

GRADE 3

1. *dull*—Too little sleep makes a *dull* mind.
2. *bank*—The *bank* of the river was changed by the flood.
3. *again*—Please show me *again* how to tie the knot.
4. *picture*—Sue's *picture* had three little ducks in one corner.
5. *these*—We can use *these* balls in our marble game.
6. *oil*—Love is like *oil* that keeps things running smoothly.
7. *eggs*—Three *eggs* hatched in the robin's nest.
8. *share*—We enjoy our blessings more when we *share* them.
9. *tomb*—Jesus' *tomb* was empty on Easter morning.
10. *quarter*—Each one may have a *quarter* of the sandwich.
11. *Mrs.*—Did you give the card to *Mrs.* Landis?
12. *planning*—Jacob was *planning* to gain the birthright.
13. *next*—When will the *next* term begin?
14. *Lord*—The *Lord* controls the storm.
15. *rainbow*—The *rainbow* faded away in a few minutes.
16. *bought*—I *bought* enough seeds for your garden and mine.
17. *can't*—George *can't* quite reach the top shelf.
18. *Job*—The Book of *Job* has forty-two chapters.
19. *heavy*—How *heavy* is a hummingbird egg?
20. *lawn*—Rosa's *lawn* is bordered with flowers.
21. *covers*—This platform *covers* a deep well.
22. *finger*—Henry's *finger* was swollen from a bee sting.
23. *handle*—Always *handle* your Bible with reverence.
24. *world*—All the riches of the *world* cannot bring happiness.
25. *goat*—A young *goat* is called a kid.

GRADE 4

1. *west*—The sun sets in the *west* each night.
2. *body*—The sick boy's *body* is very weak.
3. *bench*—This *bench* is so slippery.
4. *roots*—The fig tree dried up from the *roots*.
5. *ladder*—One rung of the *ladder* is broken.
6. *heap*—The feed bags are on a *heap* on the floor.
7. *branches*—He trimmed *branches* in the orchard.
8. *stories*—Lois read two *stories* aloud.
9. *becomes*—As water freezes, it *becomes* ice.
10. *wanted*—The dog *wanted* another bone.
11. *health*—We thank God for *health* and strength.
12. *ordered*—Mother has *ordered* new shoes.
13. *instead*—We ate crackers *instead* of bread.
14. *heaven*—Jesus looked to *heaven* and prayed.
15. *shipped*—Grain is *shipped* across the ocean.
16. *Saturday*—One *Saturday* it rained.
17. *later*—We ate *later* than usual.
18. *schoolhouse*—The *schoolhouse* will be empty.
19. *robin*—A young *robin* flew from its nest.
20. *seventeen*—"Jacob lived in . . . Egypt *seventeen* years."
21. *marbles*—Four *marbles* are lost.
22. *animals*—Some *animals* hibernate all winter.
23. *all right*—Is it *all right* if he comes?
24. *greatest*—Obeying God is our *greatest* duty.
25. *week*—On the first day of the *week*, Jesus arose.

GRADE 7

1. *enrolled*—The hospital secretary *enrolled* my name.
2. *brethren*—A group of *brethren* discussed the plan.
3. *initial*—Your *initial* try may not succeed.
4. *mediator*—A good *mediator* will be impartial.
5. *sacrifice*—Some people *sacrifice* their health.
6. *resurrection*—A *resurrection* of reading began.
7. *credible*—Is your reason for tardiness *credible*?
8. *admonition*—Isaac heeded the *admonition* given.
9. *annually*—Robins generally fly south *annually*.
10. *commitment*—His *commitment* to quality is kept.
11. *proclaim*—The Jews would often *proclaim* a fast.
12. *attitude*—Glen knelt in an *attitude* of prayer.
13. *indicate*—Budding trees *indicate* springtime.
14. *requirements*—What *requirements* are needed?
15. *interview*—Newsmen often *interview* the president.
16. *apparent*—Was this *apparent* burglary reported?
17. *conscience*—To sin willfully dulls a *conscience*.
18. *advantageous*—It was *advantageous* to farmers.
19. *century*—Life in our *century* keeps changing.
20. *mobile*—Our lower jaw is *mobile*; it is not fixed.
21. *agitate*—Do not *agitate* this muddy water.
22. *beneficial*—Most snakes are *beneficial* to man.
23. *feasible*—Joshua gave a *feasible* plan of action.
24. *impelling*—A wind is *impelling* our boat to shore.
25. *attraction*—Samson's *attraction* to her hurt him.

GRADE 8

1. *infallible*—God's prophecies are *infallible*.
2. *enthusiastic*—Balaam was *enthusiastic* about rewards.
3. *perished*—He *perished* with the Midianites.
4. *suspicion*—Habitual honesty keeps one clear of *suspicion*.
5. *anticipation*—Live with *anticipation* of eternity.
6. *evangelist*—Paul was a traveling *evangelist*.
7. *malicious*—He faced *malicious* persecution.
8. *acquaintance*—Develop *acquaintance* with the elderly.
9. *preceding*—*Preceding* experiences gave them wisdom.
10. *instinct*—Birds migrate by *instinct*.
11. *conveniently*—Can you *conveniently* mail my note?
12. *protein*—A dog needs *protein* in its diet.
13. *procedure*—Use a consistent training *procedure*.
14. *miniature*—Grandfather carves *miniature* furniture.
15. *advisable*—It is *advisable* to keep his knife sharp.
16. *ceremony*—Visitors appeared without *ceremony*.
17. *eligible*—Who is *eligible* for the prize?
18. *scheme*—Our gardening *scheme* was successful.
19. *assurance*—Goliath had a false *assurance* of power.
20. *efficient*—David was *efficient* with his sling.
21. *financial*—Credit cards bring *financial* snares.
22. *dedicate*—We will *dedicate* this poem to Grandmother.
23. *literature*—She enjoys our *literature*.
24. *indefinite*—We saw *indefinite* forms in the fog.
25. *civilized*—Cultivate *civilized* manners.

FINAL TEST

CONTINUED

GRADE 5

26. *purse*—I will look in my *purse* for a Band-Aid.
27. *headache*—All the smoke gave him a *headache*.
28. *barrel*—Is the biggest *barrel* empty?
29. *capitol*—Men meet in the *capitol* building to make laws.
30. *bishop*—The *bishop* preached the sermon.
31. *fought*—The muskrat *fought* to free himself.
32. *baptize*—The Ethiopian asked Philip to *baptize* him.
33. *Christian*—Thank God for *Christian* parents.
34. *object*—Circle the *object* of the preposition.
35. *finally*—Dinner is *finally* ready.
36. *policeman*—Ask the *policeman* where Route 10 is.
37. *safety*—Fasten your *safety* belts.
38. *worship*—We gather for public *worship* at church.
39. *declare*—The people of God *declare* His glory.
40. *postage*—How much *postage* does a letter need?
41. *except*—No one saw it *except* Mother.
42. *awfully*—Grandfather's leg pained him *awfully*.
43. *drawn*—That man has *drawn* many pictures.
44. *potatoes*—Peas and *potatoes* make a good meal.
45. *hadn't*—I *hadn't* seen anyone behind me.
46. *pleasure*—She accepted the invitation with *pleasure*.
47. *froze*—The blossoms *froze* in the late frost.
48. *guide*—A map is a good *guide* for travelers.
49. *Creator*—We worship the *Creator*.
50. *expect*—We *expect* Jesus to return any time.

GRADE 6

26. *insurance*—The *insurance* building burned down.
27. *especially*—That was *especially* kind of you.
28. *guard*—The Jews set a *guard* at the tomb.
29. *disappear*—Problems *disappear* through prayer.
30. *who'll*—I don't know *who'll* come.
31. *source*—God is the *source* of all good.
32. *bruise*—There was a small *bruise* on her face.
33. *hygiene*—We study *hygiene* in health class.
34. *assured*—He has *assured* me that all is well.
35. *percentage*—What *percentage* is my profit?
36. *happiest*—He was the *happiest* one there.
37. *choir*—The shepherds heard an angelic *choir*.
38. *prophesy*—Did Isaiah *prophesy* of Christ?
39. *vice-president*—The *vice-president* was busy.
40. *exactly*—Do *exactly* as I tell you.
41. *qualified*—She is well *qualified* for the job.
42. *accept*—God did not *accept* Cain's sacrifice.
43. *exclaimed*—"Help me!" *exclaimed* Frank.
44. *calendar*—Please change the *calendar* page.
45. *honestly*—We must make our living *honestly*.
46. *auditorium*—The *auditorium* had three hundred fifty seats.
47. *etc.**—The word *et cetera* means "and so forth."
48. *Phil.**—The pupils memorized *Philippians* 4:8.
49. *exam**—This *examination* is nearly over.
50. *mm**—The cardboard was one *millimeter* thick.

GRADE 4

26. *year*—One *year* has twelve months.
27. *cookies*—Are the *cookies* all eaten?
28. *wool*—Clothes made of *wool* are warm.
29. *aren't*—The books *aren't* new any more.
30. *pudding*—We ate chocolate *pudding* for dessert.
31. *different*—Use a *different* color.
32. *holiday*—What was the last *holiday* we had?
33. *remove*—God told Moses to *remove* his shoes.
34. *cents*—Peas cost five *cents* more than beans.
35. *weather*—Warm *weather* helps crops grow.
36. *led*—The shepherd *led* his sheep home.
37. *chase*—I watched the cat *chase* the butterfly.
38. *awhile*—You may rest *awhile;* that will refresh you.
39. *quickly*—Jesus said, "Behold, I come *quickly*."
40. *presents*—Wise men gave *presents* to Jesus.
41. *cookbook*—Look in the *cookbook* for the recipe.
42. *good-bye*—He waved *good-bye* and rode away.
43. *built*—The wise man *built* his house on a rock.
44. *hungry*—If your enemy is *hungry,* feed him.
45. *chief*—My *chief* desire is to live for God.
46. *Fri.**—After Thursday is *Friday.*
47. *Gen.**—The first book of the Bible is *Genesis.*
48. *mo.**—January is the first *month.*
49. *in.**—One-twelfth of a foot is an *inch.*
50. *km**—One thousand meters is a *kilometer.*

GRADE 7

26. *solution*—Judas found no *solution* to his problems.
27. *interrupt*—Did I *interrupt* your conversation?
28. *extension*—Please plug in the *extension* cord.
29. *complicated*—An infection *complicated* matters.
30. *dependent*—Its pressure is *dependent* on depth.
31. *redemption*—The *redemption* price is very costly.
32. *difference*—Does it make any *difference* to you?
33. *consequently*—I was ill; *consequently* I slept.
34. *involved*—The long trip *involved* much planning.
35. *circumstances*—None chose his *circumstances.*
36. *convenience*—Leon found the ramp a *convenience.*
37. *admission*—Judas's *admission* did not save him.
38. *gradually*—His bricklaying *gradually* improved.
39. *negotiations*—Legal *negotiations* take months.
40. *endeavor*—She will *endeavor* to do right.
41. *Incarnation*—The *Incarnation* was miraculous.
42. *patriarch*—Abraham was a respected *patriarch.*
43. *affiliate*—He was a business *affiliate* of Lewis.
44. *feminine*—Karen has a fragile *feminine* appearance.
45. *junior*—Mr. Smith needed a *junior* business partner.
46. *cassette*—Dan put a *cassette* into the tape player.
47. *mosquitoes*—Only female *mosquitoes* will bite.
48. *opportunity*—Study nature at each *opportunity.*
49. *superstition*—Is her fear from a *superstition?*
50. *discipline*—They have good *discipline* in school.

GRADE 8

26. *inconvenience*—Frozen pipes cause major *inconvenience.*
27. *energy*—Direct your *energy* into useful channels.
28. *occurred*—An eclipse *occurred* during the battle.
29. *vague*—Don't be *vague* with your suggestions.
30. *recommend*—Can you *recommend* an improvement?
31. *precious*—An honest friend is a *precious* treasure.
32. *occasional*—You will face *occasional* misunderstandings.
33. *frequently*—Do not *frequently* analyze your friend's trust.
34. *crusade*—The neighbors staged a *crusade* against litter.
35. *certainty*—No one has the *certainty* of tomorrow.
36. *superintendent*—A *superintendent* must be on time.
37. *testimony*—Your hobbies are a *testimony* of your interests.
38. *career*—A farming *career* takes many skills.
39. *bouquet*—My lilac *bouquet* drooped quickly.
40. *exhibition*—Orderly children are an *exhibition* to the world.
41. *tendency*—Resist the *tendency* to slouch.
42. *preparation*—Good meals take *preparation.*
43. *criticism*—We cannot cure faults by *criticism.*
44. *stampede*—Thunder triggered the *stampede.*
45. *refugees*—Storm *refugees* stayed in the school.
46. *temporary*—It was a *temporary* shelter.
47. *peaceable*—Did everyone have *peaceable* neighbors?
48. *separately*—Part of the order will be shipped *separately.*
49. *sanctify*—Prayer will *sanctify* your thoughts.
50. *canoe*—Keep your *canoe* out of the rapids.